CURRICULUM AND TEACHER EDUCATION

CURRICULUM AND TEACHER EDUCATION

edited by

*Professor Muhammad Hamid Al-Afendi
and Professor Nabi Ahmed Baloch*

HODDER AND STOUGHTON

KING ABDULAZIZ UNIVERSITY, JEDDAH

British Library Cataloguing in Publication Data

Curriculum and teacher education. –
  (Islamic education series).
  1. Islam – Education
  2. Education – Curricula
  3. Teachers, Training of – Islamic countries
  I. Al-Afendi, Muhammad Hamid
  II. Baloch, Nabi Ahmed
  III. King Abdulaziz University   IV. Series
  375   LC905.C/

ISBN 0 340 23609 4
First printed 1980
Copyright © 1980 King Abdulaziz University, Jeddah

Printed in Great Britain for Hodder and Stoughton Educational, a division of Hodder and Stoughton Ltd., Mill Road, Dunton Green, Sevenoaks, Kent by Hazell Watson & Viney Ltd, Aylesbury, Bucks

Preface

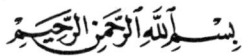

In order to realize the aims and objectives of Islamic education it is necessary for schools, colleges and universities to have an Islamic curriculum. But a curriculum and even the text-books prepared according to that curriculum cannot make education truly Islamic either in spirit or in practice if the teachers are not faithful Muslims and if they do not know the proper methods of teaching according to that curriculum. Curriculum and teacher education are thus closely interlinked.

Curriculum always reflects the concept of Man that the society believes in, the ideology and culture that it inherits or has acquired or intends to preserve and the goal that it wants to achieve. The liberal education that Muslim countries have either accepted from the West or have felt compelled to follow for political or worldly reasons, is at present highly confused in ideals and ideologies and greatly indecisive in its aims and objectives. This state of affairs reflects the loss of a basic norm that the society is suffering from. Muslim society has not as yet lost that norm, but Muslim scholars have not as yet succeeded in integrating that norm with all the new dimensions of knowledge that come from the West. As a result a section of the community has preserved its traditional Islamic curriculum for a traditional system of education. At the First World Conference on Muslim Education held in Mecca in 1977 there was an attempt to remove that cultural duality by suggesting a new classification of knowledge. But this was an initial step. Even this has to be assessed and worked out in detail, the basic philosophy stated in clear terms and a new curriculum designed. Some suggestions have been made in the articles in the Curriculum section of this book.

As has been stated, even if scholars succeed in publishing an acceptable curriculum, detailed teacher-education plans and programmes will be needed. To obtain tutors who could train the teachers every Muslim country would have to provide dedicated, faithful specialists. These by themselves cannot achieve anything unless experts in each branch of knowledge indicate the methods to be followed in order to achieve the desired goal. Thus teacher education can be reformed only when Muslim scholars succeed in formulating Islamic concepts and suggest ways of making students conscious of them. Certain concrete suggestions have been made by some scholars, but Muslim countries can apply them only when work in conceptualization and text book writing has gone ahead.

Training in any particular branch of knowledge is, however, only one aspect of teacher education. Teacher education is total education with specialization in the methodology of teaching any one or more disciplines. The basic goal of teacher education is therefore the same as that of all education: the production of good, righteous men and women. They should be trained to be leaders and ideally be models of virtue. This requires conscious cultivation. The most outstanding historical example of that model is the Prophet of Islam and the principles of conduct are derived from what he said and did. But these have to be integrated into the curriculum of teacher education both overtly through courses in ethics and religion and indirectly through various other courses mainly in humanities. Teacher education curriculum thus needs re-examination and restructuring. It is at the same time necessary for authorities in Muslim countries to look into the entire system of teacher-education. Only then will it be possible for authorities in different Muslim countries to make the system Islamic in character.

This book initiates discussion on these two essential subjects and it is expected that scholars and authorities will make concerted efforts to solve the problem.

Syed Ali Ashraf
General Editor

Contents

Part 1   Curriculum

Edited by Professor Muhammad Hamid Al-Afendi

Introduction — Towards Islamic Curricula

Islamic Education

If we study the Holy Quran closely we should be able to formulate a workable integrated curriculum with a unique philosophy and methodology. The Quran attaches paramount importance to everything that concerns education and philosophy. It deals with the genesis of creation, the creation and the basic nature of man; it analyses the existing social order, the work of nature and stresses the urgent need for man's spiritual edification.

The ultimate objective which Islamic education has in view is the creation of good and righteous individuals who will lead happy and fruitful lives in this world and aspire, through good deeds, to achieve spiritual bliss in the hereafter.

The principles and rules which govern man's life in this world and the next are not entirely left to circumstance or man's individual reasoning. Man's life is intended to be regulated by God-given laws inferred from the Quran. Allah says, 'Nothing have We omitted from the Book'. (Chap. 6, verse 38).

Since education is of vital importance in guiding the lives of people, its philosophy and basic principles must be derived exclusively from

3

the Holy Quran instead of being left to the discretion of educationists who are subject to all manner of unwholesome influences.

Alien systems having failed to provide an appropriate education for the individual and society in the light of Islam, it is high time Muslims turned to the Holy Book and the Sunnah of the Prophet for Islamic educational theory.

Modern education differs from the Islamic in that it is built on two hypotheses. It does not recognize the supremacy of religion and it seeks to divorce religion from life.

Islamic education is different. It attaches considerable importance to religious matters as well as to everyday problems of life and living.

Islamic education does not regard life as an end in itself. Life on earth is but a bridge which man must cross before he enters into spiritual life after death. Herein lies a fundamental difference between modern and Islamic education. Modern secular education merely considers happiness in this world as its final goal, whereas Islamic education regards life as only a means of achieving happiness in the hereafter. This basic difference in the aims and objectives of modern and Islamic education leads to differences in the methods by which these aims and objectives are achieved.

Modern education seems to consider everything that brings comfort and prosperity in this world as conducive to happiness. In other words, it is solely preoccupied with achieving worldly happiness by utilizing any means available. On the other hand Islamic education sees the happiness of man as fundamentally based on intellectual, emotional and spiritual convictions. Spiritual happiness in this world prepares for a life of everlasting happiness in the next.

The segregation of the religious from the secular in non-Islamic educational systems is reflected in the policies of educational institutions and the functions, aims and objectives of schools and universities. Thus there are state schools and ecclesiastical schools functioning separately.

In Islam there is no segregation between religious and secular education. They are inseparable and indivisible. Neither aspect should be over-emphasized at the expense of the other.

The basic differences between Islamic and secular education are currently neglected or frequently overlooked by those working in the field of education throughout the Muslim world. The political and economic instability of many Muslim countries, seen against the background of the political supremacy, material progress and indus-

4

trial and economic advancement of non-Muslim countries, has apparently alienated Muslims from the principles and teachings of Islam. It has led them to believe that by merely copying, borrowing or transplanting non-Islamic education systems, they can match the progress already achieved in non-Muslim countries.

Often the systems imitated are travesties of the principles of Islam. Muslims have not achieved the hoped-for material and political progress, nor has this education satisfied their desires or answered their innermost religious feelings.

A distorted Picture

Education has been split into two distinctive types, modern and religious, which are independent of and irreconcilable with each other in non-Islamic countries. Modern education has its own schools, institutes, colleges and universities, as has religious education. This duality or artificial division is entirely at variance with the principles of Islam.

It is a situation which urgently demands an immediate and drastic change in the existing curricula now in force in educational institutions in most Muslim countries.

Abolition of Duality in Education

Duality in education must be abolished immediately. Any segregation between religious and secular issues should be eliminated. Scholarly specialization in any field is futile and inadequate in the building up of one's personality unless one is on terms with both the secular and the religious aspects of life.

5

The Aims and Objectives of Islamic Education

The ultimate aim of Islamic education lies in the inculcation of the concept of Allah in the minds and souls of God-fearing individuals. In order to achieve this, Islamic education is divided into what is called individual and social education. Individual education aims at familiarizing the individual with:

   (a) his relation to other creatures;
   (b) his individual responsibilities in life;
   (c) his reponsibilities towards the human community;
   (d) his social relations;
   (e) his relationship to the universe and universal phenomena and exploration of nature's laws in order to utilize and exploit them;
   (f) his Maker's creative wisdom apparent in His creation.

We can draw up an Islamic curriculum comprising all these components on the basis of the Holy Quran.

(a) The Concept of Allah

The first item which Islamic education curricula should strive to inculcate into the minds of the young is the concept of Allah. Young Muslims should be sufficiently acquainted with the omnipotent and pervading power of Allah and His divine attributes. Allah is the Creator of this universe and the Lord of the Worlds. He is the educator of the entire Creation. We should dedicate our thanksgiving and worship only to Him. There is no god but He and none should be worshipped but He. To Allah we shall all return, and with Him we seek shelter. He is the First and the Last, the Transcendent and the Immanent.

The concept of Allah and His divine attributes are repeatedly referred to in the Holy Quran.

It is a very comprehensive concept that embraces the whole range of life on earth.

(b) The Individual Personality

Allah says in the Holy Quran, 'Behold! Thy Lord said to the Angels, I am about to create man from clay. When I have finished him (in due proportion) and breathed into him of my spirit fall ye down in obeisance unto him'. (Chap. 38, verses 70–71).

From this Quranic verse we can infer that man is made up of matter and spirit, which are interdependent. Therefore, Muslims reject the materialistic concept of man which views man only as a material entity composed of physical and chemical components. Muslims also reject the concept which regards man as a purely spiritual creature.

The human entity is one and indivisible.

As matter and spirit are closely interrelated so are thought and action, worship and living, idealism and realism. Therefore Islamic curricula should focus on the unity of man and the integrity of his personality. Man is superior to animals but he is not perfect or infallible.

The Status and Prestige of the Individual

Allah says in the Quran, 'Behold, thy Lord said to the Angels, "I will create a vicegerent on earth". They said, "Wilt Thou place therein one who will make mischief therein and shed blood, where we do celebrate Thy praises and glorify Thy holy (name)?" He said, "I know what ye know not". And He taught Adam the nature of all things. Then he placed him before the angels. They said, "Glory to Thee. Of knowledge we have none, save what Thou hast taught us." He said, "O Adam! tell their natures". When he had told them, God said, "Did I not tell you that I know the secrets of heaven and earth, and I know what ye reveal and what ye conceal"?' (Chap. 2, verses 30.33).

Man is Allah's vicegerent on earth. He is able to teach and learn despite the fact that he can be corrupt and shed blood. Those who are corrupt and shed blood need proper education and proper guidance. Anyone who teaches well, learns well, and worships Allah sincerely is striving to be worthy of his position as God's vicegerent on earth. Allah says, 'We have honoured the sons of Adam, provided them with transport on land and sea, given them for sustenance things good and pure, and conferred on them special favours above a great part of Our creation.' (Chap 7, verse 70).

Individual Responsibility

Allah says in the Holy Quran, 'Not one of the beings in the heavens and the earth but must come to (God) Most Gracious as a servant. He does take an account of them (all) exactly. And everyone of them will come to Him singly on the Day of Judgement.' (Chap. 29, verses 93–5).

Islamic curricula should primarily be concerned with the education of the individual whom God has honoured and for whom the fruits of life were created for his sustenance. Man should aspire to the status he was created for.

Such an individual will be brought up to abide by Allah's orders and thank Him for the many good things Allah has offered him. Allah says, 'Every soul draws the meed of its acts on none but itself. No bearer of burdens can bear the burden of another.' (Chap. 6, verse 164). In another place Allah says, 'Every man's fate we have fastened on his own neck. On the Day of Judgement we shall bring out for him a scroll which he will see spread open. (It will be said unto him) 'Read thine (own) record: Sufficient is thy soul this day to make out an account against thee.' (Chap. 17, verses 13–14).

Islamic curricula cultivate and promote individual responsibility. Whoever does good is rewarded for his good deeds and whoever does evil is duly punished. No one is responsible for the deeds of others. It is only those who sin who are punished for their sins, not their substitutes nor representatives.

Guided Individual Freedom

The curricula of Islamic education guide the individual and teach him how to distinguish between evil and good, the forbidden and the permissible. Furthermore, they allow him full freedom to think, decide for himself and choose whichever way he should seek. Allah says in the

Holy Quran, 'O children of Adam! Wear your beautiful apparel at every time and place of prayer. Eat and drink, but waste not by excess, for God loveth not the wasters' (Chap. 7, verse 31).

To be appropriately and unobjectionably dressed in a presentable and respectable manner is a habit which ought to be cultivated and encouraged among the young who, when brought up to adhere to the principles of cleanliness and good manners, will live up to such principles and will in the long run form a nation infinitely rich in morality, and will be respected and commended by all other nations. Islamic education advocates the golden mean in every form, even in food, drink and clothing. Islamic education discourages all forms of excess in words and deeds. Islamic curricula should comprise any item which pertains to the betterment of the mental and physical health of the individual. They should familiarize the younger generation with everything that brings about spiritual security and content in every field of human activity, such as being well dressed for prayer, meeting people in the mosque and standing in the divine presence of Allah. If one says his regular prayers five times daily, no one will be left the slightest chance to remain unclean throughout the day. Any person who receives an Islamic education will be taught to look after his health lest he should fall sick for want of food or drink, or become overfed. The individual should be able to know different kinds of food and drink and their ingredients, and should also know the right food needed at every stage of physical growth. For this the study of medicine is quite indispensable. Allah says in the Glorious Quran, 'O ye who believe! Intoxicants and gambling, (dedication of) stones and divination by arrows are an abomination of Satan's handiwork. Eschew such (abomination), that ye may prosper.' (Chap. 5, verse 93).

Closely associated with the study of medicine and physical and spiritual health is the avoidance by the individual of all deceitful and repulsive conduct. Islamic curricula should endeavour to instil these principles into the minds of the young so that they can be brought up to hate and reject artificiality and make-believe.

Allah has given people all the good fruits of life and forbidden them everything harmful to their bodies and souls. Good non-alcoholic drink is permitted, whereas strong alcoholic drink is strictly forbidden. Alcoholic drink intoxicates the mind and deprives the drunkard of self-respect. Allah has allowed man to enjoy all the good things in life, all the pleasures he is entitled to and all that elevates the individual's soul and mind. But those pleasures of life which, if fully enjoyed by the individual, will cause displeasure, worry and sorrow, and will ultimately sow the seeds of enmity and hatred among members of the community, are undesirable in Islam and are forbidden. Other pleasures include gambling, dedication to stones and divination by arrows are degrading and dehumanizing.

Freedom of thought, inference and logic being applied to God's creation, the universe, universal phenomena and nature's secrets and laws, should all be interwoven into the curricula. Learners should be fully equipped with aids to study, and ponder over Allah's wonders and miracles in the universe. All individuals, despite intellectual differences, will eventually attain full awareness of Allah's omnipotent power observable in every living thing. Having examined the signs of Allah in the universe scientifically, logically and intellectually, the individual will certainly develop a genuine faith in Allah's omnipotence and omnipresence. Through meditation over God's creation, the individual will come closer to Allah, know Him better and will better be able to distinguish between good and evil. Man will then never stray except through arrogance and self-conceit.

Islamic curricula allow freedom of thought. No restriction is imposed on an individual's behaviour since he has already been told what is right and wrong. He who deviates from the straight path will be punished for self-deception. On the other hand he who abides by the Sharia law will never attempt to deviate from the straight path or lag behind. Moral uprightness is an absolute must and the preservation of spiritual integrity and Muslim unity is basic.

When the individual reaches the age when he will be able to shoulder all his responsibilities, he must not then degrade his mental powers. He should learn to be intellectually independent and to use his mind and refrain from being blindly led to believe in others' opinions. He should not reproduce the opinions of others in a parrot-like manner. The thinking power with which man is endowed is too precious to be wasted or misused.

Social Responsibility

Islamic curricula should promote the belief that the social order in Islam is based on unity, equality and fraternity. It rejects dictatorship and demagogism. The Muslim Ummah is one; no distinctions are drawn between Arab Muslims and non-Arab Muslims, between white-skinned and dark-skinned Muslims. Muslims, wherever they are, are united in their feelings and aspirations. If any of them is in distress others should respond sympathetically towards him. Muslims are more or less like the human body; disease in any part affects all other parts which will not function properly.

Islamic curricula should emphasize those studies and endeavour to foster cooperation among the young. A self-centred person cannot be happy socially. Cooperation must lead to the good of society as a whole as well as the good of the individual. Cooperation should help promote righteousness and obedience to Allah's injunctions and commands, and not imply transgression, evil practices and sinful acts, encroachment upon the legitimate rights of others, vengeance, aggressive alliances, occupation by force of others' territories, exploitation and the usurping of others' resources. Islamic curricula bring up both individuals and communities to appreciate and respect these principles and meticulously adhere to them.

Leniency and Consultation

Allah says, 'It was by the mercy of Allah that thou wast lenient with them (O Muhammad), for if thou hadst been stern and fierce of heart they would have dispersed from round about thee. So pardon them and ask forgiveness for them and consult with them upon the conduct of affairs' (Chap. 3, verse 159). In another place Allah says, 'That which Allah hath is better and more lasting for those who believe and put their trust in their Lord, and those who shun the worst of sins and indecencies and, when they are angry, forgive, and those who answer the call of their Lord and establish worship, and whose affairs are a matter of counsel, and who spend of what We have bestowed on them.' (Chap. 42, verses 36.8).

Islamic curricula aim at bringing up an individual who is lenient, kind-hearted and has good manners; an individual who neither maltreats nor does injustice to others, forgives those who trespass against him if forgiving is conducive to the betterment of others' behaviour. He will not bully or tyrannize over others but will consult his brother Muslims upon the conduct of affairs and will, quite willingly, abide by the majority view and work for the good of the community.

Family Relations

Allah says in the Holy Quran, 'And of His signs is this: He created for you mates from yourselves that ye might find rest in them, and He ordained between you love and mercy. Lo, herein indeed are portents for those who reflect.' (Chap. 30, verse 21).

Islamic curricula aim at preparing the young, males and females, to be good husbands and wives so that families will live in peace and family ties are further strengthened. The interpersonal relations between the members of the same family and of all the human families throughout the world rest on one concept: that all human beings are descended from Adam and Eve. The husband should seek spiritual shelter and rest in his wife and *vice versa*. They should each feel compassion and love for each other. Without this the family will not be happy. Children are better brought up in a healthy family atmosphere and will be compassionate and loving to one another. Such happy families will establish later small or large communities, all loving and all compassionate.

Social Solidarity

In a society where solidarity prevails, the individuals are bound together by ties of love. No one violates or encroaches upon the legitimate rights of others. Each does his duty to the best of his ability. The strong feel compassion for the weak, the rich for the poor. No transgression or injustice is allowed. Daily transactions among them are free from exploitation and opportunism. Islamic curricula should endeavour to foster these moral principles in theory and practice.

International Systems and Relations

Islamic curricula should embrace all the fundamental rules upon which international systems and relations are based, besides the relation of the individual to society.

The relationship between the ruler and the ruled, the counsellor and the counselled, social institutions in each country and international relations ought to be based on the public interest in every field. When the individual is brought up to respect the inviolable rights of others there will be no need for security councils and international courts; might will not be right, and tools of destruction and corruption will not be utilized. Allah says in the Holy Quran, 'Fight in the way of Allah against those who fight against you, but begin not hostilities. Lo! Allah loveth not aggressors.' (Chap. 2, verse 190). 'Make ready for them all thou canst of (armed) force and of horses tethered, that thereby ye may dismay the enemy of Allah and your enemy.' (Chap. 8, verse 60).

Islamic curricula call for reform without resort to aggression. This does not mean or imply surrender or humiliation. The Muslim believes 'Ummah' is the best that was ever created on earth. Therefore the believers should be strong, powerful, dignified. They should maintain their status, repel their enemies and be sufficiently armed to thwart and defeat any aggression. He who indulges in the foul practice of aggression will invoke the wrath of Allah; for Allah loveth not aggressors.

A country which has been the victim of aggression is fully entitled to retaliate against the aggressor and Muslims must be brought up to defend their countries against foreign invasion and to enlist in their national armies.

Allah has guaranteed that the townships of His pious and devoted worshippers will not be destroyed nor will their cities, countries and kingdoms be swept away.

Islamic curricula are responsible for the inculcation of this belief so that pupils will learn that everything is in the hands of God and God is never unjust. Allah says, 'And whosoever does an atom's weight of good will see it then. And whoso doth an atom's weight of ill will see it then.' (Chap. 99, verses 7–8).

Islam deems it necessary that all countries should respect international treaties and undertakings; otherwise no country will be able to respect itself or enjoy the respect of other countries. Living in peace and security and respecting the undertakings between individuals is equally important. Every individual should maintain the right of Allah and the rights of the people. Children should be brought up to understand and believe in this.

There are various other factors which make nations and countries live in peace, happiness, security and enjoy good neighbourly relations free from aggression or invasion. 'If the people of the townships had believed, and kept from evil surely we should have opened for them blessings from the sky and from the earth. But (unto every messenger) they gave the lie, and so we seized them on account of what they used to earn.' (Chap. 7, verse 96).

Faith and piety create happiness in the lives of individuals and communities. They account for the blessings that emerge from the earth and descend upon them from the sky. But rejection of the true faith, corruptibility and disobedience to Allah bring evil consequences. Allah says in the Holy Quran, 'Allah coineth a similitude: a township dwelt secure and content, its provision coming to it in abundance from every side, but it disbelieved in Allah's favours. So Allah made it experience the garb of death and fear because of what they used to do.' Islamic curricula should tell young pupils that enjoining right conduct, forbidding indecency and believing in Allah, account for the fact that Muslim Ummah is the best community that has been raised up for mankind. The principles which Islamic education should cultivate in the minds of the youngsters are all summarized in the verse from the Holy Quran wherein Allah says, 'Say: come, I will recite unto you that which your Lord hath made a sacred duty for you: that ye ascribe nothing as a partner unto him, and that ye do good to parents, and that ye slay not your children because of penury. We provide for you and for them and that ye draw not nigh to lewd things whether open or concealed. And that ye slay not the life which Allah hath made sacred, save in the course of justice. This He hath commanded you, in order that ye may discern. And approach not the wealth of the orphan save with that which is better till he reach maturity. Give full measure and full weight, in justice. We tax not any soul beyond its scope. And if ye give your word, do justice thereunto, even though it be (against) a kinsman; and fulfil the covenant of Allah. This He commendeth you that haply ye may remember. And (He commandeth you, saying): This is my straight path, so follow it. Follow not other ways, lest ye be parted from His way. This hath He ordained for you, that ye may ward off (evil).' (Chap. 6, verses 151–53).

Man and the Universe

Allah says, 'He hath created the heavens without supports that ye can see, and hath cast into the earth firm hills, so that it quake not with you and he hath dispersed therein all kinds of beasts. And We send down water from the sky and we cause (plants) of every goodly kind to grow therein.' (Chap. 31, verse 10).

This Quranic verse suggests many subjects for the Islamic curricula in schools and universities. For instance, the heavens which are suspended in the universe without any support, the orbiting stars and planets and the laws which govern their motions, light and darkness, life and death, day and night which are but the direct consequences of the orbiting stars and planets—all these miraculous universal phenomena indicate God's creativity and call for worship of Allah and belief in the divine attributes and nature of Allah the Almighty. The hills that are cast onto the earth so that it may quake not with people on it, the infinite mineral resources deeply laid within the bowels of the earth, the geological strata of which it is composed and the unexplored treasures they hold; the numerous creatures which live on the crust of the earth or within it; the beasts which live on the earth and the creatures which live in water, the plants which grow on the surface of the earth or within it—all these are but Allah's signs in His creation. Each sign is a sufficient proof that there is only One God and that no partner should be associated with Him. He is the Lord of the Worlds, the Maker of all creation and the only God who should be worshipped by mankind. Allah says in the Quran, 'He created the heavens and the earth with truth, and He shaped you and made good your shapes, and unto Him is the journeying.' (Chap. 64, verse 3).

Besides the study of the heavens and earth and all that is between them, Islamic curricula should focus on the study of man from all

15

angles. People should realize how they were created and given the best of shapes. The physiological study of man should concern itself with the organs of the human body and the function of each. Man should know and learn how to keep his body healthy and secure. The interrelationships between the various organs of the body should be emphasized. The study of the various organisms which jointly function to preserve the life of the human being, and the biological and physiological differences between male and female, and the wisdom inherent in the making of males and females are all indications sufficient to prove the existence and miraculous creativity of Allah, the Almighty. The secrets of life and the seeds of self-preservation have all been deposited in man. The conception and evolution of a new being is well illustrated in the Quran. The fertilized ovum develops into a foetus and finally emerges into the world where it lives and dies. Across the journey of life man is exposed to moments of strength and weakness, health and sickness, happiness and unhappiness and all that can befall man until he dies. On the Day of Judgement man will be rewarded for his good deeds and punished for his sins. This is man's inescapable destiny. Allah says in the Holy Quran, 'Lo! Allah (it is) who splitteth the grain of corn and the date stone (for sprouting). He bringeth forth the living from the dead and is the bringer-forth of the dead from the living. Such is Allah. How then are ye perverted?' Detailed methodologies should be drawn up to conform with the facts in the verses quoted above from the Quran. The universe has its own unique discipline and the laws governing its motion are infallible. Man must study natural phenomena and explore their secrets and mysteries in order to comprehend the infinitely miraculous power of the Creator. Allah did not create the universe haphazardly. Thoughtful consideration of the signs of Allah in His creation leads to staunch belief in His miraculous power. The right to receive worship is Allah's exclusive prerogative.

All such things should be minutely studied so that man can come to the full recognition of Allah's infinite power and surrender his life and soul to Him in devoted servitude.

The most significant of all objectives of education is the inculcation in the mind and soul of the individual of the concept of Allah or 'Tawheed'. Allah is divested of all material characteristics attached to living things. Allah has no parallel, substitute or partner. He is the absolute ideal of righteousness, goodness and beauty.

Social Education

To sum up, Islamic curricula should aim at the following objectives:

(1) Building a society of good, pious and God-fearing individuals where social justice prevails;
(2) Building a society where toleration, brotherhood, love, mercy, goodness and righteousness are predominant;
(3) Building a society based on mutual consultation and the maximum exploitation of the individual's intellectual capacities;
(4) Building a society where individuals enjoy freedom of thought and are competent to take responsibility;
(5) Building a society where individuals can live an ideal, pure and happy life.

Once again we emphasize that the ultimate aim of Islamic education is to bring man closer to Allah. Everything else is but subsidiary. All available means should be utilized to instil this objective deep into the minds and souls of Muslim children.

Non-Islamic curricula abound in hypotheses, pretension, falsehood, distortion and misconception which have unfortunately crept into education curricula in Muslim countries. Such infiltration has become so entrenched into the thinking of many intellectuals and educationists that it is now very difficult to defeat it or even fight it openly. Some Muslim intellectuals and educationists wholeheartedly support these misconceptions simply because they have been introduced by men like Darwin and Freud. Darwin and Freud are believed to have introduced new schools of thought, to be the harbingers and founders of new culture even though this is inconsistent with the principles and teachings of Islam.

Muslims must reconsider Islamic curricula currently applied in Muslim countries with a view to purifying them from alien elements and the gross misconceptions in which they abound. Scientific facts mentioned in the Quran and Sunnah should replace pseudo-scientific hypotheses incorporated in non-Islamic curricula.

Nevertheless, we do not advocate rigid, reactionary, narrow-minded policies. We support a full enjoyment of the pleasures and rewards of life within the dictates of Islam. Such pleasure should not alienate man from the Muslim ideal nor should this divert him from aspiring to achieve happiness in the life-after-death. Our prayer should always be, 'Our Lord! give us good in this world and good in the Hereafter, and defend us from the torment of the fire.' (Chap. 2, verse 201).

Distinctive Features in Islamic Education Curricula

Educationists who are fond of modern educational terminology and who feel attracted by apparently new educational theories will find that all that is truly Islamic is really modern, unique and genuine. The Holy Quran and the Sunnah contain many references to educational theories and methodologies which should be interwoven into the curricula of Islamic education in Muslim countries.

The following are some of the distinctive features of Islamic educational curricula:

(1) Islamic curricula create an integrated personality and prepare the individual for every aspect of life. Man should receive education through his life as education is a continuous and never-ending process. This is also current thought in modern secular education;

(2) Islamic curricula focus attention on the spiritual and material needs of the individual which are inextricably united;

(3) Islamic curricula aim at the inculcation of faith in the minds and hearts of the younger generation, the correction of morals and the spiritual edification of the soul. They also aim at the constant acquisition of knowledge, the combination of knowledge and work, faith and morality and the practical application of theory in life;

(4) Islamic curricula require that a spiritual atmosphere be established between the instructor and his disciples so that belief and surrender to God's divine will can be cultivated in the minds and souls of the learners. Modern secular methods fail to cultivate belief and faith as aptly and lastingly as when both teacher and learner are spiritually more in harmony;

(5) Islamic curricula emphasize the importance of good teacher-training programmes. Teachers should be well-chosen and should be sincerely dedicated to the teaching profession;

(6) Any person who strictly follows the principles of Islamic

18

education will become skilled in exercising his reasoning power and insight into life, and will not resort to thoughtless imitation. He will not confine himself to the ideas of his predecessors particularly if such ideas were mistaken, misconceived or distorted in matters of belief;

(7) Islamic curricula create in minds and souls the foundations of eternal happiness and constant security through belief in Allah, the unity of all mankind, discipline and hope;

(8) Islamic curricula help the individual to acquire the character of the learned 'ulama. The Muslim 'Alim (learned man) fears Allah and endeavours to acquire knowledge in every field from his cradle to his grave. He is well aware of the limitations of man, and that divine science is limitless. He does not pretend to know more than he does, but always strives to widen his scope of knowledge. The Muslim learned man studies theology, psychology, cosmography, history, archaeology, botany, agriculture, zoology, biology, ethics, astrology, statistics, mathematics, physics, chemistry, geography, geology, and above all man and how he should utilize every potential for his own good;

(9) Islamic curricula stress the value and sincerity of man's work in the cause of Allah and mankind;

(10) Islamic curricula require that man should believe in Allah and that he should be loving, righteous and compassionate toward his fellow-men. Man should be fully acquainted with truth in his incessant attempt to realize the unity of being and the unity of living;

(11) Islamic curricula gauge man's belief, morals and scholarship in the light of his sincerity and dedication to work;

(12) Spoon-feeding and memorization are not the best means of fostering education in the minds of the young. Application, and not merely theoretical knowledge, is indispensable;

(13) Islamic curricula adopt methodologies mentioned in the Quran. Such Quranic methodologies are inimitable and indispensable.

When such methodologies are applied educationists and curricula experts should consider their suitability to current circumstances.

Islamic education is a great educational revolution in its objectives, curricula and methodology with distinctive features in realism, idealism, comprehensiveness and precision.

It is time to organize Muslim education curricula on the basis of Islam so that Muslims can restore their status and well deserve the Quranic acclamation: 'Muslims are the best generation that was raised unto mankind.'

Dr. Muhammad Hamid Al-Afendi
Chairman of the Curricula and
Methods Department,
University of Riyadh.

Chapter One

The Islamic Concept of Educational Curricula

U. A. Al-Beely

Ustaz Ahmed Al-Beely has held various posts associated with religious and secular education in Sudan since 1951. He taught in secondary schools and teacher colleges. He has been head of the Department of Arabic and Religious Education, Chief Inspector of Arabic and Religious Education, Lecturer at the College of Arabic and Islamic studies in Omdurman, and Director General of the Department of Religious Studies which looks after Khalwas (Quran Schools) and Quran Institutes at all levels.

The Duality of Education

Duality of education means having two types of education with two separate aims, beginning at the primary stage. This is the case in Egypt and some other Arab and non-Arab countries. In those countries one type of education starts at the primary stage with special curricula, and ends with Colleges of Islamic and Arabic education. The graduates of this type of education usually work as teachers, mosque Imams, or preachers.

The other type of education is secular education which follows a different kind of curriculum from primary up to University level. The graduates of this type of education take miscellaneous jobs except for those which are allotted to graduates of Islamic Universities.

Duality in this sense has its supporters and its opponents, and each group has strong reasons for taking sides. These reasons are discussed below.

The advocates of duality claim that every Muslim Country is keen to keep abreast of material progress, and to attain parity in standards with advanced countries in such areas as industry, civilization and modern technology. They also claim that there is no way to attain

21

such standards except by training specialists in physical science, industry, the arts and humanities.

Modern advanced countries have followed this plan and reached a high standard in science and industry. It is therefore imperative that we, in Muslim and Arab countries, should train some of our sons and daughters to bear the responsibility of changing our countries from materially under-developed to materially advanced ones.

The only way to train specialists in physical science, mathematics and other branches of knowledge which constitute the basis of modern civilization, is to establish a graded education system which prepares students for eventual courses in Universities or higher institutes. However, such students should receive a small amount of religious education and Arabic language teaching during the pre-university stages. They could for instance learn short chapters of the Quran, religious observances, and essentials of Arabic grammar.

The supporters of duality also claim that Muslim countries should not forget, in the rush for material progress, that they have an Islamic legacy and an Arab legacy which are closely related: a unique relation between a language and a religion not to be found elsewhere at the present time. We should not, they say, in our search for modern ways of life, lose sight of our responsibility to understand both traditional legacies but study them at a highly specialized level. Since material progress is well taken care of by establishing schools, universities and higher institutes to train successive generations for the responsibility of material development, the spiritual side should also be catered for. Aims should be drawn up and the means to achieve them should be defined by establishing special schools at all levels for religious education.

The Quran in the Curriculum

Nobody concerned with Islamic education would disagree that the Quran is the Cornerstone which links the Arabic and the Islamic. Memorization of the Quran helps jurists in producing evidence, helps linguists in finding examples, and helps others interested in Islamic and Arabic studies whenever they need an authoritative reference. It also improves the style of public speakers and writers when they borrow from its elegant, inimitable words and verses.

Most Muslim countries are in greater need of knowledge to raise their material standards, but separate groups of students should specialize, some in secular subjects and others in religious subjects. The religious group could study subjects to give them sufficient knowledge of the beliefs and observances in Islam, and to improve their moral principles. They could also study enough Arabic to enable them to read with understanding, write or speak correctly, and translate efficiently from other living languages.

This group specializing in religious subjects could study an additional limited number of secular subjects, but should devote the greater part of their lives to the preservation of both Islamic and Arabic legacies; safeguarding them against any break in continuity of linguistic tradition or failure to transmit their cultural heritage to posterity, or against misconceptions of religious beliefs, observances, and laws. Some of this group should reach the stage of specialization where because of their long experience they could give independent opinions in the absence of a text (*Ijtihad*), and discriminate between the authentic and the spurious, or the true and the false.

This group will never reach a high standard unless they memorize the Quran together with the Prophet's Traditions and the sayings of their venerable forefathers. They should also add to their repertoire of literary works, prose and poetry, produced by Arab writers during the historic period of pristine purity. The memorization of such works will improve their sense of judgement, and make them efficient guides and reliable authorities on matters of religion, language, and life in accordance with Islamic principles.

This is the Islamic and Arabic legacy: these are its origins and sources and special institutions should be established for their study. Students should join them in their childhood and engage in memorizing the Holy Quran and reciting it; studying exegesis and principles of deduction used by previous religious leaders; and memorizing a large number of the Prophet's Traditions. It is difficult to provide such specialized training as is required in religious and linguistic studies at the university stage alone, as the advocates of unification at the primary and intermediate stages claim.

However, it is essential that those specializing in Islamic and Arabic studies should take, during the three pre-university stages, adequate courses in mathematics, physical science, geography and the general history of mankind; and should be given the opportunity to learn one foreign language to the level of reading with understanding. The knowledge of a foreign language is necessary for a preacher of Islam, for it enables him to read what was and is written about Islam in that language, to defend Islam against its detractors and to enrich Arabic by translating good material into it. He can preach Islam in such a foreign language among its speakers.

Refuting Arguments for Duality

I do not agree with the supporters of dual education, because it is very harmful educationally. It is possible, however, to design a curriculum which does not have the disadvantages of that followed in dual education. Such curricula can provide highly specialized training in all branches of religious knowledge, without having ill effects, educationally or sociologically, of the kind which are usually associated with duality in general education, and which never existed in any Muslim country in former times.

If we review the educational curricula of the pre-specialization stages in the light of the Islamic concept of Curriculum design, we see the educational blunder which the colonialists have intentionally committed in the Muslim East, and which we perpetuated because of our ignorance of its disastrous results. Some Muslim thinkers however still support this blunder, and even try to justify it.

Supporters of the dual education system from the primary stage were not far-sighted at all, in spite of the reasons they gave. Although I agree on the need for training specialists in religious and secular subjects, I do not agree that such specialized training as is required should start as early as the primary stage before a pupil's interests, mental abilities, and skills are adequately developed.

The Islamic Concept of Educational Curricula

First: In the early Islamic periods

Every civilized nation has religious beliefs and observances, customs and traditions, and positive laws which govern conduct among its individuals and between it and other nations.

A nation designs its educational curricula so that a favourable climate may be created for preparing future generations to learn its beliefs accept them, defend them, and become zealous for them and for the worship of God in accordance with the Commands He revealed. Educational curricula also embrace social traditions and encourage adherence to them. The laws that govern individual or group behaviour are based either on the laws revealed by God, or on social traditions and general rules which have been established and accepted by the society concerned.

These statements apply to nations which follow revealed religions as well as to nations which follow man-made religions. Consequently the curricula which are suitable for a non-religious nation cannot also be suitable for a religious one, and curricula suitable for a Christian nation cannot be equally suitable for a Muslim nation. Curricula can vary within each nation at recognized stages of education so that special training may be given to selected groups of students.

These briefly are the major factors that influence the design of educational curricula. In the light of these factors educational curricula of any Muslim nation can be examined to find out how they were designed in the past, and how they changed during periods of foreign occupation.

After the revelation of the Holy Quran had been completed, and the Prophet's Traditions had been recorded, Muslims occupied themselves with memorizing the Quran, understanding it, reciting it, and reporting the Prophet's Traditions, orally at first, and later in writing. They compiled the Prophet's Traditions under various titles and according to different methods. At that time the Muslim nation's curriculum was clearly outlined. It was based on two main pillars, the Quran and the Prophet's Traditions, and on related studies such as Islamic jurisprudence and religion, together with Arabic language studies that helped understand them. The Islamic curriculum was so influenced by God's words in the Quran and the Prophet's Traditions that it deserved to be called 'A divine curriculum for mankind'. Since the Holy Quran is the axis round which Islam revolves, Muslims put tremendous effort into memorizing it, understanding it, deducing rules from it, and obeying its commands in everything they did. This has no parallel in the case of any other book, holy or otherwise.

The Quran was the first subject children in Muslim societies learned in the *Maktab* (*Kuttab*, or *Khelwah*), after they had learned the alphabet.

Then, after memorizing the Quran, they were taught the fundamentals of Islamic religion, Arabic language and the physical sciences.

The reason why the Quran was the first subject taught to children is outlined here:

Certainly the Holy Quran is the perfect model of eloquence and rhetoric. We know that it may be difficult for children to understand most of the meanings conveyed in it; and we know that although they are taught the Quran they are never required to attempt to produce any writing in a similar style. However, the benefits gained from learning the Quran were the incentives which induced the forefathers of this nation to prescribe the inimitable holy book as the first text which the children read and wrote in the *Maktab*, and the first to leave its stamp on their hearts. Children were thus educated, from an early age, according to the divine curriculum designed for the education of mankind, from the time it was revealed to the day of resurrection. Our forefathers favoured the early teaching of the Quran because they realized that material memorized in childhood remains engraved on the mind for the rest of life, and that those who do not memorize the Quran in their childhood are unable to do so as adults. They also realized that familiarity with the Quran at an early age has its impact on the learner at later stages in his life even if he forgets some of it.

The impact of memorizing the Quran is manifested in the linguistic ability of the learner, his style, and his moral principles. At the linguistic level, the learner can pronounce his words correctly, however long or unfamiliar they are, because he practised pronouncing all the words in the Quran, and was trained to produce the various sounds of Arabic. At the stylistic level he can quote verses of the Quran in their appropriate context whether he is giving a speech or writing an article; and he can produce evidence from the Quran to support his argument against that of an opponent in a discussion or debate. At the moral level, the Quran learner reads it regularly, and comes frequently in contact with God's instructions concerning what a Muslim should do and what he should not, or with moral stories which tell him what happened to unbelievers, sinners and wrongdoers. I can say, from personal observation, not yet scientifically verified by statistical analysis, that memorizing the Quran is a safeguard against committing crimes such as theft, embezzlement or adultery. A reader of the Quran lives in so divine an atmosphere that he sees crime in its most repulsive image. Every time he is tempted to commit a sin, he immediately recalls its prohibition by God, and the repugnant image the Quran drew of it, e.g. 'Nor come nigh to adultery: For it is a shameful (deed) And an evil, opening the road (To other evils)'[1] or 'Intoxicants and gambling, (Dedication of) stones, And (divination by) arrows, Are an abomination), That ye may prosper'.[2] A research worker with the opportunity to study the correlation between crimes and the educational level of the criminals would find that almost none of the criminals had memorized passages from the Quran.

Since the Holy Quran has such a beneficial influence, it should be the corner-stone of education at all stages preceding university or entrance to higher institutes, just as it was in the early Islamic periods. It is a grave error to plan any curriculum that does not allow the majority of children to become familiar with the Quran, or that provides them with only a scant knowledge of Arabic – so enabling them to understand what they read, but not giving advanced training in correct speaking or writing, as often happens in secular schools at present.

The reasons given by the supporters of duality in education are usually the following:

1. A nation needs specialists in all walks of life and specialization should start at the primary stage of education.
2. There is an urgent need to pay special attention to the Quran, and its impact on the behaviour and education of young people.
3. Consequently it is necessary to train a group of Muslim whose primary task is understanding it so fully that they may be able to know how to draw evidence from it. What is said about the Quran applies equally to the Prophet's Traditions.

These are the reasons usually given to support the perpetuation of two types of education. Those who put them forward want education to stay as it is in most Arab Muslim countries at the moment: secular schools from the beginner's stage, and religious schools from the primary stage. This is the case in Egypt, to give an example, where there are Al-Azhar institutes and secular schools existing side by side. Some Arab countries followed the Egyptian example with a slight variance in the subjects prescribed. The Sudan, for instance, used to have two types of education, from 1912 to 1969, but attempts were made to develop similar curricula for both types after the Department of Religious Affairs had been founded in 1955. Then in 1970 religious institutes at all levels were abolished, without any effort to reform the curricula of general education according to the Islamic concept. Quran schools and one religious secondary school, were, however, kept open.

Different varieties of what is basically a dual system of education are followed in Syria, Algeria, Morocco, Saudi Arabia, and the United Arab Emirates.

Second: A brief historical account of duality and its effects

Formerly there was one general curriculum in all Muslim Countries even after the invasions of the Mongols, the Tartars, and the Crusaders. The establishment of religious institutes and secular schools side by side in the Arab and Muslim countries started only after foreign occupations in the 19th and 20th centuries. Occupation powers decided to wage war against the main cultural elements of the colonized people, but in a cunning and deceitful fashion. They planned to leave religious teaching institutes to die out gradually as nobody would enrol in them for fear of being unemployed after graduation or of getting a low salary even if jobs were available. Consequently they left Al-Azhar, Al-Zaitonna, Al-Maahad Al-Elmy of Sudan, and similar institutes, to carry on with religious education, and founded alongside them the so-called secular schools in four stages. They gave those new schools beautifully and purposely designed buildings, provided them with equipment and apparatus, and trained teachers of various subjects. Government offices were eager to employ these new graduates in various jobs. Parents saw that secular education yielded fruit in the form of respectable jobs with big salaries and so they rushed to enrol their children in those schools, while the religious institutes were left for either some of the children whose families were concerned with religion, or the children of poor families. The graduates of those institutes had no prospect of employment except as teachers of the Arabic language and religion, mosque Imams, preachers, or in a very few cases, Muslim Court Judges.

When both religious and secular types of education produced graduates in the Arab countries, the products of secular education held top positions in the armed forces, police, civil service and public administration, while the products of religious education were only employed in Islamic roles. A cultured and class struggle broke out between these two groups, and each group accused the other of being inferior. The secular graduates boasted of knowing a foreign language and of their familiarity with experimental sciences, the general history of mankind, geography, mathematics etc. The religious graduates put forward their excellent achievement in memorizing and reciting the Quran, familiarity with jurisprudence, theology and other branches of Islamic studies, as well as with linguistic science such as morphology, grammar, rhetoric and prosody.

Measures taken by occupational powers made people firmly convinced that it was only the sheikhs (ulama) who should be concerned with the study of religion and adherence to it, and that secular schools produced another type of educated people who were not expected to understand religion or to adhere to it. Consequently people in most Muslim countries suffered from that sort of dichotomy, and would forgive an Effendi[3] who did something wrong, but would not forgive a sheikh for doing the same thing, because in their view the sheikh was closely connected with religion but not the Effendi. The dichotomy created by occupying authorities is similar to the dichotomy established in Western countries where religion is completely divorced from everyday life, associated only with churches on Sundays and with priests, monks and nuns, to the exclusion of other men and women. This dichotomy is alien to Islam, because there is no clergy in Islam; there are only specialized schools of religion as opposed to laymen who do not specialize in studying religion.

The effect of duality on legislation and jurisdiction

Graduates of law schools and faculties continued what foreign rulers started in the field of legislation. They enacted laws which were not derived from Islamic jurisprudence, but from the laws of the occupying country, be it England, France or any other. Considering their educational background, those graduates could not possibly consult the original sources of Islamic jurisprudence (Sharia), because they did not study them or develop the ability to deduce laws from them and understand their terms. Even those who were familiar with Islamic jurisprudence through personal effort, were not allowed by the government to introduce Islamic laws; and moreover, if they suggested such laws and published them in books, the government would not enforce them.

Considering that teachers of subjects other than the Arabic language and Islamic religion were very much in the majority in schools, their influence was that much greater. Colonialists knew that one corrupt teacher could corrupt many, if not all, of his students. Student teachers trained as teachers in local colleges or abroad in London and Paris, were encouraged to neglect religious observances and not to worry about Muslim laws on adultery, or alcoholic drinks. When they became teachers their lax behaviour was infectious, and that is why most school leavers are not religious, while most Islamic institute leavers are religious. When higher schools and universities were founded secular school leavers and graduates came to power in all the occupied countries and consequently Islamic laws were not and still are not enforced in any Muslim country (apart from personal statutes) except in the Kingdom of Saudi Arabia, although all of the colonialists have left. This is a direct result of colonialist power: they 'brainwashed' the Muslims. It is not surprising then that brainwashed Muslims continue what colonialists started in an attempt to sever all connection between Islam and the present-day life of Muslims. It was this imminent danger that induced the authorities in the land of the two Holy Mosques (*Al-Haramain*) to present the problem to those concerned with Islamic thought, and to invite them to investigate its different aspects and suggest a radical solution which could be implemented by all Muslim countries. Some of the countries which use two different types of curriculum from the beginning of primary education have attempted to solve the problem by adding all the curricula of secular schools, in spite of their drawbacks and enormous content, to the curricula used in religious Institutes. This was not an effective remedy, because it added to the burden of the Institutes and students. Consequently they could achieve neither an adequate command in their main subjects, nor an equivalent standard in secular subjects as their counterparts in other schools. In point of fact a large number of these students made greater efforts to master modern subjects (such as physical science, mathematics and geography as distinguished from religious and Arabic studies) and neglected their main subjects, only because modern subjects led to science faculties and eventually meant respectable jobs, with big salaries and prestige. Religious Institutes therefore lost some of the bright students because nothing attracted them to stay and graduate from them.

Some countries kept both types of curricula unchanged because they believed that to be the best policy, but they also tried to attract students to religious education by offering prizes, scholarships, and other rewards.

Other countries completely abolished religious educational institutes, and decided that students selected to pursue Arabic and Islamic studies at universities should have been able to score high marks in Arabic and Religious Education in their pre-university examination. These countries kept primary, intermediate, and secondary school curricula as they were; the number of religious subjects was not increased, and no reward was provided for those students who achieved exceptionally high standards in Arabic and Religious Education. Consequently bright students made greater efforts to study those subjects that enabled them to join such faculties as law, engineering, medicine, science, and agriculture, and few students were attracted to Arabic and Islamic subjects. Islamic universities followed the policy of 'something is better than nothing', and required applicants to have passed the Secondary Education Certificate Examination and to have obtained high marks in Arabic and Religious Education.

This solution can hardly help Islamic universities to recruit students of equal calibre to those who join faculties of medicine and engineering, for example. Islamic and Arabic studies in Muslim countries will soon be delivered over to people who have not received proper training at the pre-university stages, and who became interested in those studies only because they had no chance to join faculties whose graduates obtain big salaries.

The above discussion shows that there is an urgent need to draw up an educational plan free from all the faults pointed out in the religious curricula, Muslim institutes, and secular curricula and schools. The new plan should discuss the curricula, textbooks, teacher training, school life and harmony between school life and life outside schools. That kind of harmony cannot be achieved without cooperation between the mass media and the ministries of education. We can never establish a desirable Muslim society by reforming school curricula and teacher training while the press, radio, television and the cinema are left uncontrolled, and are pouring out material ignoring the principles or the teachings of Islam.

The Right Solution

I find it necessary, before presenting what I regard as the right solution, to state some facts which should be taken into account, and identify some aims which should be achieved in every Muslim society.

The facts are:

1. All kinds of human knowledge, whether concerned with the natural science or with the humanities, have developed and branched off into special subjects. Consequently, it has become necessary to have specialists in every branch of knowledge.

2. Islamic and Arabic language studies involve a large number of diverse subjects. Every year a new economic, medical, or political issue emerges, and scholars are required to investigate and take a decision on the basis of Islamic principles and sources. Islamic studies therefore develop in the course of time, they branch off into more sub-divisions, and the reference works increase. What has been said about Islamic studies applies also to Arabic studies, and a scholar cannot become highly specialized in both at the same level.

3. A Muslim society needs secular knowledge as much as it needs a knowledge of Islam and the Arabic language, and both types of knowledge are equally indispensable.

4. Trades and industries which are necessary for a society are regarded by Islam as part of its component elements, and should therefore be mastered by Muslims as a collective duty.

5. The mastery of Islamic and Arabic language studies at a highly specialized level, whereby scholars can derive rules from the Sharia or language texts, becomes a collective duty on behalf of the whole nation.

6. Islam urges the learning of every useful subject regardless of the place of its origin or the nationality of the scholar who introduced it.

7. Islam develops in its followers a positive attitude towards knowledge and the acquisition of knowledge. It also advises one to be modest and never to overestimate what has been learnt, and it advises laymen to consult scholars. Examples of that advice can be found in such Quran verses as the following, 'Are those equal, those who know, And those who do not know[4], 'over all endued with knowledge is One,

The All-knowing'[5], and 'if ye Realize this not, ask of those who possess the Message'[6]

8. Curriculum reform for scholars, higher institutes and universities will not by itself help in building a Muslim society and bringing up Muslim individuals according to Islamic principles and criteria, if the mass media undermine what is done by the school, the curriculum, the teachers and the textbooks. The press, radio, television and the cinema should, therefore, abide by Islamic principles, lest there should be a conflict between education and mass media, and the latter destroy what the former builds.

In addition to that, the laws enforced should be based on Islamic jurisprudence.

The aims are:

1. The training of specialists in all walks of life, from simple trades to highly academic professions.

2. The acquisition of the minimal amount of religious knowledge, religious observances, and Arabic language which every citizen should acquire regardless of his level of education.

3. The acquisition by specialists in Islamic and Arabic studies of a reasonable amount of knowledge about natural sciences and humanities.

The aims stated above should be attained by Arab-Muslim societies in relation to their linguistic background, which will determine the amount of Arabic they can learn.

The aims can be attained by implementing the following plan.

Stages and Subjects

1. The primary and intermediated stages should be regarded as one general stage which is not subdivided horizontally into different types of special education, like the general secondary stage.

2. The subjects prescribed for this stage in Arab countries should be as follows:

(a) The Holy Quran (memorization and recitation)
(b) The memorization of a certain amount of the Quran as a compulsory requisite for every boy and girl.

(c) The Quran should be spaced out over nine years so that a majority of the children can learn and memorize all or most of it during that period.

(d) State prizes should be given to children who can memorize the whole of the Holy Quran.

(e) A new type of secondary school should be founded, in addition to the ones already established in Arab countries. It could be called the Islamic Secondary School, and only those who have already memorized the Quran would be admitted to it. Students in these new schools should be given monthly grants during the course. A special curriculum should be designed for these students so that they could join Islamic and Arabic studies Faculties after they have finished their course. After graduation they should be given financial rewards such as a higher starting salary and higher annual increments. Such financial inducements would certainly attract bright students to Islamic Secondary schools.

Other subjects at the pre-university stages

1. All branches of the humanities should be free from any material that conflicts with Islam, at all stages of education. There is for instance no need to study Darwin's theory of the origin of species.

2. The amount of Arabic prescribed at stages up to the end of the general secondary school (not the religious secondary stage), should be adequate to enable school leavers, who join science faculties, technical, commerce or art colleges, to read Arabic fluently with full comprehension, and to increase their knowledge of Arabic by reading original works and reference books. This aim can be achieved only by selecting the best poetry and prose texts produced in different periods and teaching students to understand and memorize them.

3. The syllabuses of mathematics and physical sciences designed for the academic secondary schools should be advanced enough to enable the leavers to pursue their studies at science faculties without difficulty. Syllabuses of the same subject prescribed for other types of secondary schools should be simpler in content.

4. Physical sciences have no place in religious secondary schools. The curriculum should, however, include, in addition to religious subjects and Arabic, the study of history, geography and a foreign

language. First year courses should be general, but the curriculum should provide for specialization from the second year.

Religious secondary leavers will certainly be the best candidates for pursuing Arabic and Islamic studies at the university stage. They will have memorized the Quran by the end of the intermediate stage, and gone on reciting and memorizing it in the religious secondary schools and colleges.

Various types of secondary schools

The religious secondary schools should be retained, along with the commercial, industrial, agricultural and academic secondary schools. Other new types could be found as the need arose in society for specialists in new branches of knowledge.

The medium of instruction

Teachers should use classical Arabic in teaching all subjects at all stages. All branches of learning would certainly benefit from such a practice that gave further opportunities to acquire a reasonable command of language in speech, writing and understanding even if the students are not specialists in Arabic.

I am not trying to be difficult or pedantic. I only mean by classical Arabic a variety of Arabic which is correct morphologically and grammatically. It is not difficult for teachers to use such a variety of Arabic if they are given enough training to use it, and are reproved if they fail to do so.

The curriculum suggested in this paper does not provide for the study of Arabic texts, morphology or grammar, after the end of the general secondary stage (High school in some Arab countries), except in schools and colleges which train specialists in Arabic. Students and graduates will however be able to increase their mastery of Arabic if they have the opportunity, before embarking on their special studies, to listen for about twelve years to classical Arabic, which is morphologically and grammatically correct.

Obviously we do not have in the Arab countries these days teachers who can present history, geography or physical sciences in classical Arabic. It is therefore necessary to organize in-service training courses for practising teachers, and similar courses for student teachers. The latter groups should seize the opportunity during teaching practice in schools to practise the use of classical Arabic. Their failure to do so should be counted against them in the evaluation of their teaching practice.

Teachers of Arabic and Islamic studies are capable of using classical Arabic in class, but they are worried in case they are branded by their colleges and students as pedantic. Their fears would be dispelled if the Ministry of Education announced that classical Arabic should be used in teaching all subjects in every period, and that the use of colloquial dialect is a crime; a teacher who did so would be punished and a teacher who used classical Arabic would be rewarded. If that was announced and made part of educational policy, teachers of Arabic and Islamic studies would be the first to implement it.

If such a measure is not taken classical Arabic could be in danger of perishing as colloquial Arabic is competing to replace it in the classroom and the home, through radio and television programmes. A foreign language becomes another rival when the children start learning it.

Language is the most important and significant component of a nation's culture. A nation which does not respect its language is doomed. Colloquial Arabic is not the language that expresses our thoughts and feelings as Arabs, nor does it preserve our religion and culture. Classical Arabic is the language which we use for all these purposes. We must therefore take all the necessary measures to promote it and make it a living language of speech and writing, and the first steps should be taken in schools.

Successful and unsuccessful students

If one assumes that the primary and intermediate stages in the Arab world constitute one stage of nine years' duration, and that it is compulsory for all children from the age of six to fifteen, obviously some will pass the examination at the end of that stage and others will fail.

Successful students will probably join different types of secondary schools including the proposed religious secondary schools. Unsuccessful students, who obtain 49% of the marks or less in the intermediate stage examination, should not be deprived of the opportunity of acquiring further knowledge which makes them more efficient in the jobs they take. It should be noted that at the end of the intermediate stage the children are about 15 or 16 years old and that is too early an age for a full-time manual or intellectual job. It is for the benefit of these children that different technical, military and police institutes, suitable for various Muslim and Arab communities, should be founded. Such vocational and technical institutes as these can train soldiers, policemen, carpenters, blacksmiths, radio and television repair electricians, car mechanics, builders, plasterers, house painters and other tradespeople.

Students who fail the general secondary stage examination

These could join higher technical institutes where they could be trained to be foremen, skilled labourers, or teachers in intermediate technical institutes. Students who pass that examination could join university faculties.

University graduates

I think that an examination should be held at the end of the second university year, and only those who pass should be allowed to pursue their courses, which should be sub-divided into Honours and Ordinary courses. This is a system which is followed in some European and Arab universities. Honours degree graduates may be appointed demonstrators, then lecturers and professors. Ordinary degree graduates (who get very good, good or just pass grades should be given suitable jobs outside the university. Those who fail the proposed examination should leave the university and pursue their studies, if they wish, in an appropriate higher institute.

Arabic and Religious studies for non-specialists

Since every Muslim should know a certain amount of religion and Arabic, without having to be a specialist, it is necessary therefore to design a special curriculum of Arabic and religious studies for students who join higher technical institutes after the intermediate stage. The aims of that curriculum should be: to provide the students with essential knowledge about religion and religious observances; to train them to abide by the rules of Islamic behaviour, and to help them achieve enough command of Arabic to use it independently for the acquisition of more information about different branches of knowledge.

The curriculum suggested for the non-specialists should provide for the continuity of Quran memorization and recitation, and the study of the Prophet's Traditions. It should also contain a course devoted to the study of the doubts raised against Islam, and the superstitions, misconceptions, heresies and lies wrongly attributed to Islam.

This group of citizens is badly in need of correct information about their religion so that they do not fall prey to people who spread subversive ideas, or who trade in religion when they are really false sufis or atheists.

Quran Institutes and University Quran Faculties

Quran studies include such subjects as recording, calligraphy, narration, and exegesis, and a whole department should be devoted to them in the Sharia Faculty; or even a special faculty should be founded and called the Quran Faculty like that founded by the Islamic University in Medina.

There are students who would like to devote all their lives to Quran studies but we shall also be in need of qualified teachers to teach the Quran and its recitation. There is an urgent need, then, for opening a pre-university Institute of Quran studies which accepts all students who come to the Arab countries from Asia and Africa and have already memorized the Quran, as well as those students who successfully pass the intermediate stage examination and obtain high marks in Quran studies even if they obtain low marks in other subjects. This type of institute is more suitable, too, for the blind.

Such categories of students as have been mentioned above should be admitted to a Higher Institute of Quran Studies, as in the Sudan, and take a six year course of training. They could be called upon to lend a hand in teaching religious subjects in primary and intermediate schools. Out of respect for the Quran and its learners they should be given as high a salary as the graduates of four-year course faculties. Quran students should be encouraged; otherwise there will be no continuation of narration in respect of the Quran which can be traced back to our prophet, God bless and salute him. After graduation, those students who obtained high grades could be appointed teachers in state schools, and those who obtain low grades could be appointed Muezzins or mosque porters. The latter might also help in teaching Quran recitation to adults who missed the opportunity in their childhood.

Girls' Schools

Reforms suggested above apply also to girls' schools and women's teacher training colleges, including those for post-intermediate students. Another type of school may be added, however, in the case of girls. Mother care institutes should be founded for the benefit of girls who do not wish to join general secondary school after they finish the intermediate stage.

The curriculum designed for mother care institutes should include such studies as Islamic jurisprudence related to family affairs, and domestic science necessary for mothers and housewives. Quran memorization and recitation, Prophet's Traditions and life story, as well as other general subjects deemed necessary for girls, should be continued at these institutes.

Quran Institute for Girls

Special institutes for girls should be founded for teaching Quran subjects such as recitation, narration and reading, since Quran memorization and recitation is not exclusively for men. Women graduates of these institutes could teach the Quran in girls' state schools, or join universities and pursue other Islamic studies such as jurisprudence, Traditions, and theology. In all cases they should enjoy the same concessions as their male counterparts. This type of institute is also suitable for blind girls.

Graduates of these institutes may also help in teaching adult women reading, writing, and short chapters of the Quran for memorization according to recitation rules. A 'literacy for women' campaign would be very helpful.

The need for training in manual skills

Contempt for manual work is a dominant attitude in the Arab world. University graduates are often helpless when it comes to fixing small things they need in their daily life, and they have to seek the help of skilled labourers in these matters. In order to change this attitude, and develop a respect for manual work as well as teach graduates useful manual skills which will help them to fix and repair small things without feeling that it is below their dignity to do so, the intermediate and secondary school curricula should, in my view, include training in basic carpentry, electrical engineering and mechanics. Every effort should be made inside the school to show respect for manual work and the people who do it to earn their living.

Obviously, some manual skills are more suitably acquired by boys, whereas others are more suitable for girls.

A Final Word

The textbook is the most important educational tool, since it is the student's companion at home and at school. The spirit of Islam should, therefore, be the dominant feature in all textbooks on different subjects. Moreover all our courses, books and teaching materials should have as their central theme the relationship between God, man and the Universe. It should be stressed that God always gives and man receives, God is worshipped and man is the worshipper. The universe is intended by God for the service of man so that man can worship God. Man needs help and God created the universe to help man.

Theological studies are about God.

Humanities are about man.

Natural studies are about the universe.

Textbook writers, teachers, and learners should always remember these relationships between God, man and the universe, and should always draw attention to them and stress them, so that we may always worship God, believe in Him alone, and refer to his Shariah only for decisions on every new issue in our lives.

When this is done, the Muslim world will not be the same as it is now. We shall then discover our latent powers, release them, become worthy of shouldering the responsibility that was left for us to bear, and rise to fulfil our mission, which is the propagation of Islam in the whole world. 'And my success (in my task) can only come from God, In Him I trust, and unto Him I look'[7] And my last words are: 'Praise be to God, The Cherisher and sustainer of the Worlds'[8].

40

Appendix 1 —*Distribution of periods for the primary school*

Subjects	Number of Periods						
	1st Year	2nd Year	3rd Year	4th Year	5th Year	6th Year	Total
Holy Quran	6	6	6	6	6	6	36
Jurisprudence	1	1	1	1	1	1	6
Sira, Traditions and Manners	1	1	1	1	1	1	6
Reading	5	6	6	4	2	2	25
Composition	–	–	–	1	1	1	3
Grammar	–	1	1	1	1	1	5
Dictation	–	–	1	1	1	1	4
Library	–	–	–	1	1	1	3
Literary Texts	–	–	1	1	1	1	4
Handwriting	–	1	1	1	1	1	5
Science	–	1	1	1	2	2	7
Mathematics	2	2	3	3	3	3	16
Geography	–	–	1	1	2	2	6
Citizenship and History	–	–	1	1	2	2	6
Art	1	1	1	1	1	1	6
Physical Education	1	1	1	1	1	1	6
Total of weekly periods	17	21	26	26	27	27	

Notes:

1. Parts of the Quran prescribed for memorization should be first explained to learners in simple language and made easy for them to understand.
2. Jurisprudence is taught in accordance with the School of Law (Mazhab) which is predominant in the country concerned.

Appendix 2: *Distribution of periods in the preparatory school*

Subjects	Number of periods		
	1st Year	2nd Year	3rd Year
Jurisprudence	3	3	3
Beliefs	1	1	1
Sira and Traditions	2	2	2
Quran memorization and Recitation	2	2	2
Exegesis	1	1	1
Reading	2	2	2
Composition	1	1	1
Grammar	2	2	2
Dictation	1	1	1
Handwriting	1	1	1
Literary Texts	1	1	1
Library	1	1	1
Foreign Language	6	6	6
Science	5	5	5
Mathematics	6	6	6
Geography	2	2	2
History	2	2	2
Art	1	1	1
Physical Education	2	2	2
Total number of weekly periods	42	42	42

Note:

Schools at this stage should be called 'Intermediate Schools' as they used to be called by some Arab countries, since it is an intermediate stage between the primary and the general secondary (the latter used to be called High Secondary in some countries). The certificate given at the end of this stage should be called the General Education certificate since the learners do not start any specialized courses of study before it.

Appendix 3: *Distribution of Periods for the secondary school for Arabic and Islamic studies*

Subjects	1st Year General	2nd Year Ar. Studies	2nd Year Is. Studies	3rd Year Ar. Studies	3rd Year Is. Studies
Jurisprudence	2	2	1	2	1
Beliefs	1	2	–	2	–
Sira and Biographies	1	1	1	1	1
Narration and Composition of Traditions	1	2	1	2	1
Quran Memorization	1	1	1	1	1
Rules of Quran Recitation	1	1	–	1	–
Exegesis	1	2	1	2	1
Reading	1	–	1	–	1
Composition	1	1	1	1	1
Grammar	2	1	2	1	2
Rhetoric	1	1	1	1	1
Morphology	1	–	1	–	1
Lit. Texts and Hist. of Lit.	1	1	2	1	2
Library and Research	1	1	1	1	1
Foreign Language	7	7	7	7	7
Science	3	3	3	3	3
Mathematics	3	3	3	3	3
Geography	4	4	4	4	4
Citizenship and Sociology	2	2	2	2	2
Military Training	2	2	2	2	2
Hobbies	2	2	2	2	2
Total number of weekly periods	42	42	42	42	42

Ar. = Arabic   Is. = Islamic

Notes:

1. Distribution of subjects and periods for other types of secondary schools should be decided on the basis of the aims of each type. In the case of science and mathematics schools, for example, more periods should be allotted to those subjects, whereas in

43

the case of secondary schools for commerce, agriculture, or industry more emphasis should be laid on those subjects selected for specialization.

2. Students in other types of secondary schools should be given a reasonable amount of comparative Islamic Jurisprudence.

3. Schools at this stage should all be called Preparatory Schools because they prepare students for a higher stage, either University or higher institutes education. The certificate given at the end of this stage should also be called the Preparatory Certificate.

4. The Secondary School for Arabic and Islamic studies branches off into two sections after the first year. One section prepares its students for joining faculties of Arts or the Arabic Language, and the other prepares its students for joining the Faculty of Shari'ah or similar faculties.

NOTES

1. Sura Bani Israel, The Holy Quran: Text Translation and Commentary, by Abdullah Yusuf Ali, Published by Dar Al-Arabia, Beirut, Lebanon, (968, p. 703).

2. Sura Al Maida, *op. cit.* pp. 270–271.

3. Effendi, although Turkish in origin, was used for some time in some Arab countries, particularly Egypt, with reference to people educated in secular schools, and wearing Western clothes, as opposed to the rest of the citizens.

4. Sura Zurrar, Verse 9, Yusuf *op. cit.*, p. 1239

5. Yusuf *op. cit.*, p. 579, Sura, Yusuf, Verse 76.

6. Yusuf *op. cit.*, p. 667, Sura Nahl, Verse 43.

7. Sura Hud, XI, Verse 88, Yusuf, *op. cit.*, p. 538.

8. Sura Yunus, Yusuf, *op. cit.*, p. 486.

Chapter Two
Curricula of Muslim Education

Ahmed Shalabi

Dr Ahmed Shalabi: Professor and former Chairman, Department of Islamic History and Civilization, University of Cairo, Egypt. Egyptian. Dr Shalabi born in Cairo, Egypt, 1915, was educated in Egypt and England; he received his Doctorate from Cambridge University. He started his professional career as a lecturer at Al-Azhar University and then taught at the Dar-al-Ulum College, University of Cairo. He taught at the Universities of London and Cambridge and the Universities of Indonesia, Sudan, Malaysia, Kingdom of Saudi Arabia and Libya. He has also held administrative posts at the Institute of Islamic Studies, the Institute of Arabic Studies and Research, and the Institute of Diplomatic studies. He has over fifty books to his credit, the most prominent being: *The Encyclopaedia of Islamic History.* 10 vols (Arabic) edited; *The Encyclopaedia of Islamic Civilization.* 10 vols (Arabic) edited; *Comparative Study of Religions.* (Arabic); *Islam Belief, Legislation and Morals.* (English); *History of Muslim Education.* (Arabic/English). Many of his books have been translated into other languages including Indonesian, Turkish, Urdu, French and Persian.

Once we attempt to consider the Curricula of Muslim Education, we inevitably find ourselves compelled to refer to the Islamic concept of learning and knowledge. The glorious Quran, without doubt, has elevated learning and held it in great esteem. This is clearly illustrated and verified even in the first of the two chapters of the Holy Book which emphasizes the worth and significance of both the written and the spoken word. In the First Revelation which deals with the spoken word Allah addresses the Prophet, and says: 'Proclaim! (or Read) in the name of thy Lord and Cherisher, who created, —Created man out of a (mere) clot of congealed blood' (96:1–2)

Other Quranic verses follow in abundance, emphasizing the remarkable excellence of learning and the unequalled prestige of the 'ulama'. Among these verses are the following:

(a) 'There is no God but He: that is the witness of God, His angels and those endued with knowledge standing firm on justice'; (3:18)

(b) 'Say: 'Are those equal, those who know and those who do not know?'; (39:9)

(c) 'God will raise up, to (suitable) ranks (and degrees), those of you who believe and who have been granted (mystic) knowledge;' (58:11)

The Prophet (God's blessings be upon him) said in this connection:

(a) Seek knowledge from the cradle to the grave.
(b) He who honours the learned (Ālim) has honoured me.
(c) On the Day of Judgement the ink which the learned men use in writing their works will be equal in value to the blood of the martyrs.

For the first time in the history of mankind Islam made it imperative for every individual to seek knowledge, that being the first and indisputable right man is entitled to exercise. With the emergence of Islam, this right, which formerly used to be the exclusive preserve of priests, was publicly announced and stressed in this Quranic verse, 'It is not necessary for all believers to go out in *jihad*; why does not a contingent come out of them, devote themselves to studies in religion, and admonish the people when the people return?' (9:122). In this way all Muslims become both teachers and learners. Islam attaches great importance to education and the Muslim Concept of education is so broad and comprehensive that it embraces both the philosophy of education and the theories about educational organization. Islamic civilization has long and ancient traditions. It attaches considerable importance to the growth and development of various aspects of man throughout his brief span of life. Educational institutions including universities and schools expanded and grew in number, and palaces, bookshops, the homes of the 'ulama' and literary saloons were virtually converted into schools. Arab Bedouin habitations were as important as centres of learning as mosques. But whereas the study of the Arabic language flourished among bedouin tribes, all kinds of studies were pursued inside the mosques. In Islamic education a text-book was considered to be of great significance; its authority was undisputed, so that libraries in several Muslim countries became centres of learning.

According to the Islamic concept of education learners should, in the ceaseless pursuit of knowledge, come into closer contact with teachers and not rely mainly upon text-books. More important still was the urgent necessity of providing the learner with a proper methodology so that he could not only become a learned man but also be able to communicate his thoughts to students with ease and clarity.

Islamic education stressed the value of close co-operation between the school and the home in the up-bringing of the child. It also stressed the necessity of academic degrees, punishments and incentives, teachers' tuition fees and clothes, teachers' associations, equal opportunities for all Muslims to seek and acquire knowledge, and vocational and academic guidance of students, according to their individual potentialities or inclinations.

Muslim thinkers spoke about educational endowments and subsidies, the various stages of education, educational tours and female education. Muslim philosophers were very much concerned with the kindergarten and the inculcation of Muslim thinking into the child's mind.

The acquisition of knowledge presupposes a deep acquaintance with, and a close examination of, diversified curricula but I believe that the current Curricula of Islamic studies are far from being up-to-date. If one looks carefully into the curricula of Islamic studies now in vogue in our religious universities, one will see that they are borrowed wholesale from Al-Azhar university. True, Al-Azhar stood firm against the impenetrable darkness of the Middle Ages. Even before it was firmly established it had long resisted and challenged Western Colonialism; but, battling with so much trouble and misfortune, Al-Azhar could only survive. Growth and development were scarcely attainable goals. With the emergence of the contemporary cultural renaissance in the Muslim world and the establishment of colleges and universities, university policy-makers looked to Al-Azhar for guidance, applied its curricula and even borrowed the names of its faculties and departments. Al-Azhar curricula were automatically transferred to the new universities which also attracted the graduates of Al-Azhar to teach in the faculties affilitated to them. Seldom do we find an Islamic university anywhere in the Muslim world which does not employ Al-Azhar graduates to lecture on Islamic studies. Any Al-Azhar graduate delivering a lecture to his students, cannot refrain from referring to and using curricula he has been familiar with at Al-Azhar, the parent religious institution of the Muslim world.

For nine years I too received my education at Al-Azhar University. I was industrious, keen on my studies and I always came first among my colleagues. But what did I study? What information did I gather during those nine tiring years? On what intellectual lines were the curricula of Al-Azhar based? What would be the result if a comparison were made between the curricula of Al-Azhar and those of Cairo, Cambridge or London University?

No true comparison can be made, yet Al-Azhar, for well over a thousand years, spared no effort to safeguard and promote Islamic studies despite the serious and often insurmountable problems it had to face. On the other hand, Al-Azhar, like the newly established

Islamic faculties and universities, is blameworthy for not keeping pace with change and for being content with, and working along, the same old traditional lines.

At Al-Azhar I studied many jurisprudential and legal questions such as polygamy, divorce, inheritance, slavery and the like. I was also made familiar with the general Muslim opinion on such matters, but I never learnt the philosophy of Islam in dealing with such questions and controversies. Neither the Sheikh (teacher) nor the old references mentioned one single word justifying Islam's viewpoint as regards the acceptance of polygamy or divorce and the strict adherence to the inheritance or slavery disciplines. Being thus completely unarmed, I found myself unable to defend Islam against those who considered polygamy a social disaster, divorce as being destructive of the family; and argued against the justice of not equating man with woman in matters of inheritance or allowing the evil practice of slavery. Only when I began, in Europe, to study legislation of other religions and to compare it with that of Islam, did I realize what I had missed at Al-Azhar.

In 1961 law number 103 was issued mainly to promote and develop Al-Azhar. It was not an entirely unexpected law. To my mind, this law must have been primarily intended to weaken Al-Azhar; for it allowed exceptional students to study medicine, engineering and agriculture, whereas the less gifted students had to join the original religious faculties. Consequently, graduates of religious faculties, less brilliant as they were intended to be, are not likely to become the leading Muslim thinkers of the future.

If our present-day generation of 'ulama' have achieved some progress in the field of Islamic studies it is because they never had any other alternative. Had they had the chance to join the faculty of medicine or engineering they would not have hesitated to become doctors or engineers, leaving their jobs as research workers in the field of Muslim thought.

The modernization of Al-Azhar did not, however, touch the basic structure of the Curriculum. The out-moded and traditional curricula remained unchanged with the inevitable result that Al-Azhar and most of the other religious universities laboured heavily under the burden of the past.

The rejuvenation and modernization of the curricula of Islamic studies can be accomplished only if the syllabuses are enriched with the new courses such as comparative religion, Islamic civilization in its modern sense, comparative jurisprudence which properly places Islamic legislation among legislation in the rest of the world, along with the writings of historians and men of letters. The revitalization of Islamic curricula is a further contribution to the philosophy of thought in the sense that Islamic jurisprudence will not have to be studied as a separate entity without taking into consideration the aims it aspires to attain.

A further improvement to Islamic curricula will be made if some items which modern thought no longer requires or accommodates are abandoned, such as the over-exaggerated hypotheses mentioned in some books on Islamic jurisprudence, particularly in chapters dealing with divorce and cleanliness, or the allusions to Hebrew history with which books of Tafsir (commentary) are crammed. Development can also be achieved if books on Islamic studies are remoulded, rewritten and presented in an attractive, lucid and unambiguous style which suits the intellectual and linguistic requirements of the contemporary world.

Ethics, in the purely Islamic sense of the term, should deal with morals and values; unfortunately it now leans more towards purely philosophical controversies. Consequently, it has lost its clarity of vision, and become more ambiguous, unintelligible and misleading.

I would like, in a few words, to enumerate those drastic and necessary changes that should be made when the curricula of Islamic studies are drawn up:

(1) The introduction of some courses such as comparative religion and Islamic studies, provided that highly competent committees clearly define the content of these syllabuses lest they should turn out to be new philosophies.

(2) The modification of the principles and methodology of teaching Islamic history.

(3) Thoughtful reconsideration of the teaching material of Muslim jurisprudence.

(4) The omission of allusions to Hebrew history which were purposefully introduced into some subjects.

(5) The revising of Islamic textbooks in an attractive, unambiguous style in keeping with present day requirements and curricula.

Comparative religion is a subject which was unknown before the emergence of Islam but the Quran referred to it in this verse: 'And dispute ye not with the people of the Book except with means better (than mere disputation)'; (chap. 29, verse 46). Unbiased and harmless disputation means the exposition and discussion of religious controversies logically and objectively so as not to be misguided by philosophical complexities and ambiguities.

Since the dawn of Islam the 'ulama have taken an interest in comparative religion and made worthy contributions in this new field. Among these were Al-Noubakhti (died in 202 A.H.), Al-Masoudi (346 A.H.), Al-Masihi (420 A.H.), Al-Baghdadi (429 A.H.), Ibn Hazm (456 A.H.), Al-Shahristani (548 A.H.), and many others.

Many non-Muslims were converted to Islam after a thorough and conscientious study of comparative religion, and after getting vexed questions settled for good, such as those related to divinity, miracles and prophecies, the holy book, legislation, monasticism and the place of woman.

As a purely Islamic subject, comparative religion was abandoned for reasons known only to its scholars and advocates. But before it disappeared from our curricula, it had been taken over and promoted in European institutions to be discreetly utilized later as a deadly weapon against Islam itself. And even when Muslim scholars wanted to restore it they had to go to European universities to study under the supervision of Western professors and orientalists. Nevertheless we could achieve a lot by reintroducing it.

Islamic civilization is basically the parent subject of all Islamic studies since it brings into prominence all that Islam has offered to mankind. Though Islamic civilization has dwindled now into a barren and fragile facade, in its unique and original sense it retains the following:

(1) Islamic (Creative) civilization. It deals with many questions such as those of Muslim opinion in politics, economics, education, sociology, peace and war, and many aspects of human life.
(2) Pre-Islamic (Restored) civilization: this is the civilization which was prevailing before the advent of Islam but which pined away and died until Muslims came along and restored, developed and added to it. It is sometimes called experimental civilization. Its contribution is discernible even now in the fields of medicine, mathematics, astrology, agriculture and music.

The term, Islamic history, was for long deceptive and misapplied. It covered the history of Muslim Arabs only, and sometimes only in part. In its modern sense Islamic history is so comprehensive that it now traces the history of all Muslims throughout the Muslim world back to the early days of Islam. Not completely irrelevant to Islamic history are some important studies such as the philosophy of historiography, the question of whether or not the historian should be committed to the era and society in which he lives, and the lines according to which history is to be written. In its modern and wider sense, Islamic history should highlight the contributions each individual Muslim country has made in the interest of its own people and of humanity at large in the fields of economics (agriculture, industry, trade), health, education, internal security and defence.

The study of Islamic jurisprudence should be related to the philosophy behind Islamic legislation. Comparative jurisprudence, as an independent subject, ought to be introduced into our curricula, but only after all forms of hypotheses and exaggerations have been omitted.

This is a brief survey of the Islamic curricula currently applied in faculties and universities devoted to Islamic studies.

In Muslim non-specialized faculties and institutions students must be offered courses which will ultimately foster and deepen religious consciousness. It is completely unfair to let the starving prospective doctor, engineer or accountant, exist on the very little which is offered to him before he joins the university. Religious consciousness among students of secular faculties can be fostered in the following manner:

First: Islamic civilization should be briefly studied in all faculties and by all students, Muslims or non-Muslims.

Second: Aspects of Islamic civilization ought to be dealt with in detail in faculties and institutions where different schools of thought are studied. This can be done in the following manner:

(a) A self-contained Islamic curriculum dealing with matters of politics and administration should be introduced in the faculties of political science. We should really be ashamed of ourselves when we attend, in the faculties of political science, lectures on different ideologies including the destructive ones, and ignore or underestimate Islam's wonderful achievements in the field of politics. Muslim political theory and practice, which teachers often ignore and of which most students are ignorant, can always provide a model on a sounder and more solid basis for the good of mankind.

(b) Muslim economic theory should be an integral part of the curriculum in all faculties of commerce. It is wrong that students should be forced to study all prescribed economic theories which have proved inapplicable and impracticable, in disregard of Muslim economic theory upon which a sound, co-operative and prosperous society was once built.

(c) Muslim theories of education should be introduced in the curricula of all faculties of education and educational institutions where attention has for so long been focussed on the study of Greek and British theories of education. Muslim students have long been unfamiliar with Islamic educational theories which contributed to the building of an immense volume of knowledge at a time when others could hardly write.

(d) The social theory, as Islam conceives it, should be introduced into the curriculum of social work institutions. It would provide social workers, each in his own areas of specialization, with a considerable amount of knowledge about the family and society.

(e) Al-Jihad (fighting for the cause of Islam) and Muslim military disciplines should be prescribed in all Muslim military schools and academics. The student, who is familiar with Jihad and military disciplines and strategies in Islam, will be guaranteed the best of this world and the next. Moreover, he will acquire better and richer experience in drawing up war strategies, in military engagements on the battlefield and in anticipating the consequences of wars.

(f) Muslim judicial systems including Hisba and grievances must be introduced into the curricula of schools of law and police colleges. There is no doubt that Islam's contributions in these fields laid down legal and administration foundations which are still borrowed and imitated.

(g) Priority should be given to Islamic civilization in Muslim institutions which produce diplomats and civil servants so that they can, each in his own position, grasp the genius of Islam and talk about it when occasion demands.

(h) Muslims played an enormous role in bringing back to life the pre-Islamic civilization to which we have previously referred. They restored the heritage of ancient civilizations and saved it from being lost in the midst of medieval darkness. Muslim scholars were not content with translating this heritage into Arabic. They studied it closely and did some original work in all scientific fields. In medicine, physical sciences, mathematics, astrology, music and geography, the role of Muslim scholars cannot possibly escape the notice of any research worker. Western students have been keen and enthusiastic disciples of Muslim teachers. This is clearly stated in the first volume of my eight-volume *Encyclopaedia of Islamic Systems and Civilization*.

For the above-mentioned reasons Muslim students of medicine, engineering, agriculture, mathematics and music must be well aware of the achievements Muslim scholars have made in these spheres. They should also be familiar with outstanding Muslim scientists about whom Western students probably know more than Eastern students. Among these scientists are:

(1) In medicine and pharmacology:
Al-Razi, Ali Ibn Al-Abbas, Al-Zahrawi, Ibn Rushd, Ibn Sina, Ibn Zahr.

(2) In physical sciences:
Jabir Ibn Hayyan, Al-Rozi, Al-Kindi, Ibn Al-Haithan

(3) In mathematics:
Omar Khayyam, Al-Khumarazmi, Al-Khazin, Jabir.

(4) In astrology:
Al-Ghazzawi, Al-Bairouni, Al-Mattani.

(5) In music:
Said Ibn Sojah, Ibn Mihriz, Al-Mousili, Ikhwan Al-Safaa, Ibn Bajah, Al-Tousi.

(6) In geography:
Al-Muiaddisi, Al-Istakhri, Al-Idrisi, Al-Zarqali.

In conclusion, let me draw the attention of all Muslims to the deplorable condition which we have created for ourselves by forsaking our glorious heritage and borrowing from others. Such behaviour could have been justifiable during the time when Muslims were reeling under the heavy blows of aggressors and colonialists, for the oppressed always try to imitate the oppressor. Having now regained much of our lost strength it is high time that we explored our heritage, adhered to our civilization and brought back to life this enormous and resourceful motivating force which ignorance and subjugation have strangled.

These suggestions are meant to help educational planners to draw up curricula for Muslim education. I do believe that sounder and better curricula will one day find their way into our schools and universities. All I hope is that sincere efforts will be made to speed up this process. All who contribute to this marvellous work will naturally be doing a good service to man, who will find no better guide than Islam.

Translated from Arabic by
Muhammad Abdul-Majid Barghout.

53

Chapter Three

Islamic Education: A Means Towards Self-Actualization

S. A. Abu Aali

Saeed Ateyya Abu Aali was born in 1942 in Ghamid, Saudi Arabia. Saudi. He received his Ph.D at the University of North Carolina, U.S.A. and was Assistant Professor of Education, King Abdulaziz University, Mecca, Jeddah until 1977. Currently, he is Director of Education, Eastern Region, Ministry of Education, Kingdom of Saudi Arabia.

A lesson in self-actualization through Islamic education can be obtained from the story surrounding the conversion of Omar Ibn al-Khattab the Second Kalifa after Muhammad's (peace be on him) death. One day Omar, full of anger and antagonism towards Muhammad and his followers, prepared to do battle. After all, Muhammad (peace be on him) had paid no heed to him but had given a new message to Omar's tribe. The tribal idols were attacked as worthless and Quraysh's[1] leadership in the Arabian peninsula was threatened. All these were highly significant affairs to Omar's way of thinking. He set off through Agyad in Mecca to see his sister Fatima Bint al-Khattab, a convert to Islam, to teach her a lesson she would not forget, and to persuade her to revert to the religion of her forefathers. Full of determination Omar not only wished to have his sister 'come to her senses', but have all the followers of Muhammad (peace be on him) do the same. When Omar reached his sister's home and knocked at the door, two thoughts crossed her mind: he is a misguided non-believer who mocks her beliefs; and he is her brother.

Experiencing these two emotionally contradictory feelings she opened the door. She could not help but sense his cruelty and also reel under the heavy blows he aimed at her. Warm blood started to flow down her face, but she was ready to accept any punishment in the cause of her religion.

The sight of blood on his sister's face gave Omar cause to ponder

54

his actions. His conscience was awakened and confused thoughts raced through his mind and conflicting questions presented themselves. He commanded his sister to give him the Quran which she had been reading so that he could see for himself what it was all about. But she would not obey his command as he must wash and purify himself prior to touching the Quran. She brought him water and showed him how to do this. The first words he read were: 'Taha, we did not offer you the Quran to be a cause of suffering . . .' He then asked where he could find Muhammad (peace be on him) so he could declare his conversion to Islam. He then went to the home of Ibn Abi al Arkam where he presented himself to Muhammad (peace be on him) and became a Muslim. . . . Only then did Omar realize the importance of Islam to his new life. He began to develop a sense of mission and a desire to help spread his newly acquired religion in order to earn his membership in the society of believers. For his own self-assurance, Omar asked Muhammad (peace be on him) if his followers were on the right path in this life and the hereafter, to which the Prophet replied in the affirmative. At this point Omar requested the Prophet and other Muslims to proceed to the Ka'aba to spread the word of truth to others.[2]

Arising from this historical incident, Omar began to know his true self as never before. He began to look realistically at his abilities, his points of weakness and strength. He began to see himself as a vital part of the universe that surrounded him. This is what has been labelled *self-actualization*. It is also a goal which all schools of thought in education seek to achieve, or even come close to. Since the Islamic message has brought about this self-actualization in individuals prior to and after the conversion of Omar, it continues to be a high priority goal for Muslim educators throughout the ages.

From this plateau, it is our purpose to study some of the ideas which have been mentioned in the Holy Quran and which help accomplish this self-actualization for every Muslim.

Modern educational theories and practices indicate that the functions of the school as a social organization can be summed-up as: transmitting heritage and shaping it to suit the needs of the day; and self-actualization of the individual, who is the nucleus of the society, so that he may utilize his talents and capabilities in the service of his society by improving his educational, social and material status. The individual can thus participate to the full in his responsibilities as a citizen (which include cooperation with other citizens, loyalty to the authorities, as well as protection of public property and defence of the country).

In order to reach self-actualization, it is important to specify what is meant by the following terms: *Universe, Man* and *Knowledge.*

Comprehensiveness of the Message

It might be useful at the outset if it is made clear that the Message of Islam is comprehensive, suited to all people, at all times, and all places. It was not meant to be directed towards any particular group of people in any particular location. Evidence for this can be derived from the following Quranic passages: 'Blessed is he who sent down the Criterion to his servant, that it may be an admonition to all creatures.'[3] 'Say: O men! I am sent unto you all.'[4]

The Message of Islam seeks to establish a comprehensive, interdependent, and compassionate society, where every part thereof feels the pain, sorrow, and joy of each of the other component parts. Muslim society is not isolated, for it interacts with other societies affecting it and being affected by it.

Thus, the following principles are essential to Muslim society and cannot be attained unless the school meets its responsibilities towards assisting students attain their self-actualization: purification of the soul; and having bonds based on brotherhood, justice, equality love, and compassion.

The Glorious Quran says: 'It is He who has sent amongst the unlettered an apostle from among themselves, to rehearse to them his signs, to sanctify them, and to instruct them in scripture and Wisdom, —although they had been, before, in manifest error.'[5] and also says 'We sent thee not, but as a Mercy for all creatures.'[6]

The responsibility of the school rests in making these principles a reality. When this happens, the comprehensiveness of the Message becomes obvious in matters of worship, belief, and daily interaction.

The Universe

The real and the ideal merge at one point and continue side by side. There is no conflict or contradiction between the two. The universe which we inhabit was not created in vain, as Allah has shown us in this passage: 'We created not the heavens, the earth, and all between them merely in (idle) Sport. We created them not except for just ends; but most of them do not understand.'[7] In order to inhabit the earth and to fulfil the message for which man was sent to earth, a Muslim must know the features of the universe. 'Behold! In the creation of the heavens and the earth, and the alternation of Night and Day, —there are indeed Signs for men of Understanding, —men who celebrate the praises of God, standing, sitting, and lying down on their sides, and contemplate the (wonders of) creation in the heavens and the earth, (with the thought): "Our Lord! not for naught hast thow created all this! Glory Thee! Give us salvation from the Penalty of the Fire — " ',[8] Change, not fossilization, is in the nature of the universe. 'Praise be to God, Who created (out of nothing) the heavens and the earth, who made the angels, messengers with wings, —two, or three, or four (pairs): He adds to Creation as He pleases: for God has power over all things.'[9] God has placed this universe at men's disposal: 'He has made subject to you the Night and the Day; the Sun and the Moon; and the Stars are in subjection by His command: verily in this are Signs for men who are wise. And the things on this earth which He has multiplied in varying colours (and qualities): verily in this is a Sign for men who are wise. And the things on this earth which He has multiplied in varying colours (and qualities): verily in this is a Sign for men who celebrate the praises of God (in gratitude). It is He Who has made the sea subject, that ye may eat thereof flesh that is fresh and tender, and that ye may extract therefrom ornaments to wear; and thou seest the ships therein that plough the waves, that ye may seek (thus) of the bounty of God and that ye may be grateful. And he has set up on the earth stabilizers lest it should shake with you; and rivers and roads; they ye may guide yourselves; and marks and sign-posts; and by the stars (men) guide themselves.'[10]

Man

In Islamic belief, all men descend from the same origin: 'O mankind! reverence your guardian-Lord, who created you from a single Person, created, of like nature, his mate, and from them twain scattered (like seeds) countless men and women; —Reverence God, through Whom ye demand your mutual (rights), and (reverence) the wombs (that bore you): for God ever watches over you.'[11] Man was created in the best of moulds: 'We have indeed created man in the best of moulds.'[12] What distinguishes man from other creatures is his ability to control his environment. As an intelligent creature, he is required to do all he can to express himself through his presence on earth. Man's responsibility rests in that he has to control the natural forces and utilize them to his benefit and in order to avert their dangers.[13] If the first purpose for man's existence in this manner is the worship of God, he is also responsible for improving and developing his educational, social, and economic standards in order to fulfil the first objective. He, therefore, is responsible for working towards the public good or interest: 'A.L.M.R. These are the Signs (or Verses) of the Book: that which hath been revealed unto thee from thy Lord is the Truth; but most men believe not.'[14]

All Muslims are equal. The universe, the race, and the language do not represent any additional assets nor detract from a Muslim's worth. They are mere appearances which help man in realizing his human characteristics and qualities. Those who feel that they are better than others due to differences in language, race, colour, or national origin do not relate to Islam even in a remote way. True worship of God is the only distinguishing characteristic between people: Arabs and non-Arabs; men and women. It is to be understood, however, that men and women are to be differentiated on the basis of their social roles, with regard to the nature of their daily work, raising and taking care of children, and biological functions. But in all of these men and women perform complementary functions.

Although a Muslim is a member of the larger Muslim society, he has his personal freedom and rights as an individual upon whom God conferred the gift of mind and reason. The Muslim society has to do its utmost towards its own self-realization by offering a social model in which are presented practical solutions to all social, economic, political, and social organizational problems, as well as limits of responsibility or rights of a ruler or those of a citizen. This is what might be called a society of the middle nation: 'Thus have We made of you an *Ummat* Just balanced, that ye might be witnesses over the nations. . . .'.[15]

Knowledge

So that this society of the middle nation may become a reality, man has to add to his knowledge that which will help him reach self-actualization which is essential for Man's role as God's vicegerent on earth. Search for knowledge and acquiring it give meaning to Man's existence. Failure to meet this responsibility will make man indistinguishable from other creatures. Interaction between Man, other creatures, and Man's environment cannot happen without acquiring knowledge, building and developing it. God has endowed Man with the ability to comprehend, understand, and distinguish thoughts and things: 'We said: "Get ye down all from here; and if, as is sure, there comes to you guidance from Me, whosoever follows my guidance, on them shall be no fear, nor shall they grieve." '[16]

The student of Quranic studies and of the Traditions of the Holy Prophet, as well as of Islamic history, distinguish the following as sources of knowledge for Muslims: Revelation, Self, World, Nature, Experience, and History. The Muslim individual has to seek and build up his store of knowledge from these sources by utilizing what God has given him in the form of an inquiring mind. Human knowledge has progressed due to two factors:

First: Incidental, which comes in the course of normal daily routine. This type of knowledge is not subject to scientific explanation and is not connected to any social framework.

Second: Organized, which results from premeditated and planned investigation. It is subject to observation, evaluation and scientific interpretation. Epistemologists divide knowledge into three kinds[17]:

A. facts and principles, which take up the largest share of our school curriculum, generally speaking;
B. necessary methodology for absorbing facts and principles. This is

what takes up the largest share of the post-elementary level in our curriculum; and

C. the knowledge of techniques required for attaining a specific goal or objective. This knowledge is organized and requires pre-thinking and pre-planning. It does not seek to increase one's knowledge nor is it directed towards human happiness. This type emphasizes the know-how and pays little attention to the know-why. Although it is closely related to the development of a student's mental talents, it seems to be almost non-existent in Islamic schools which appear to concentrate on the first two types at all educational levels. The school in any society has to meet the two following objectives:

(a) service to the society through meeting its various needs, and

(b) meeting the needs of the individual and directing him towards the self-chosen life-style within the confines of prevailing social values.

Additionally, Muslim schools are required to meet the following objectives:

(i) Participation in building a comprehensive interdependent society built on moral principles, side by side with material progress through which an individual can grow, enjoy his rights and perform his responsibilities towards his society. Thus a society can improve and avert problems and crises that might interfere with its design for freedom and happiness of the individual. This all can be attained through education of the young. When and where this is done, a school will have given a practical example of how an Islamic school can meet its responsibilities towards humanity.

(ii) Merging the past, present, and future into one in a practical visualization of life for Muslims. What makes the Islamic curriculum distinctive is that the past is full of Islamic instructions which have established social values, and a heritage which contains many examples of the ways individual and social dilemmas and problems have been solved. The present is co-existent with present-day problems. Dealing with them makes it necessary to turn to the past in order to examine the basis of Muslim beliefs and use it as a guide. The future cannot be anything but an extension of the past, with its richness of thought, and present experience.

(iii) Preparation of the individual so that he would feel aware of his existence, self-worth, and society and feel proud of his membership of Muslim society.

(iv) Directing the individual towards his future. This is not limited to life on earth but also to the Hereafter. Therefore, the Islamic school has the responsibility of affording the student that which helps him in this life and assures happiness in the Hereafter. This life is not a goal of the Islamic school but a means towards the Hereafter. In order to attain these goals, the following proposals are advanced as a work plan for a school in Muslim society:

First: Muslimization and modernization of educational planning: all those responsible for education in Muslim countries should keep in mind the teachings of Islam when planning the curricula, and remember that this planning should meet the needs of the day. This will enable our youth to have peace of mind and also equip them to prepare for a society that serves all humanity.

Second: Preparation of educational curricula should receive careful attention, as should the organization and administration of schools, teaching methods and aids, with the objective of assisting the student in his growth.

Third: Preparation of curricula contents in a way that assists the student in discovering his abilities and utilizing them for his self-actualization. This can be accomplished through understanding the underlying principles of the curriculum and through participation in curricular development in a manner conducive to meeting the needs of present-day social problems and social development.

Fourth: Assisting the student in developing the talents of originality and innovation through encouragement of free thinking, analysis and discussion.

Fifth: Assisting students to offer their personal experiences in school environment, encourage their talents and satisfy their curiosity. Research, analysis, and evaluation ought to govern the relationship between students and their teachers.

Sixth: Instilling self-confidence and pride of belonging in students.

Seventh: Including vocational-technical training as a basic segment of the curriculum, while emphasizing the value of work and the contributions of workers in building the society. Particular care should be given to vocational education in a way that enables the student to discover his vocational abilities and to plot his future work.

Eighth: Care for all students and particularly handicapped ones who should receive special attention.

Finally, it is emphasized that Islamic education, with its outlook towards the universe, towards man who is responsible for inheritance of the earth, and towards the method of acquiring knowledge, which includes research, analysis, addition, and evaluation, is a means to self-actualization of the individual and to realization of the importance of co-operation in society.

Translated from Arabic by
Dr. Ahmed El-Afendi.

NOTES

1. Quraysh was the tribe from which both Muhammad (peace be on him) and Omar descended.
2. Dr. Ibrahim Hassan, *History of Islam*. Part 1. Cairo: Al Nahda al Misreyya Publishers 7th printing, 1964. pp. 209–210.
3. Sourah al Fourqan, 1.
4. Sourah al A'araf, 158.
5. Sourah al Jumuah, 2.
6. Sourah al Anbeya, 107.
7. Sourah al Doukhan, 38–39.
8. Sourah al Omran, 190–191.
9. Sourah Fattir, 1.
10. Sourah al Nahl, 12–16.
11. Sourah al Nisa'a, 1.
12. Sourah al Tein, 4–5.
13. Dr. Saeed Ateyyah Abu Aali, *A Study of Educational Objections In Secondary Stage in Saudi Arabia*. Unpublished Ph.D. Dissertation, Summer 1975, p. 20.
14. Sourah al Baqara, 38.
15. Sourah al Baqara, 143
16. Sourah al Baqara, 38
17. Arthur W. Foshay, 'Utilizing Man's Experience: The Quest for Meaning', *Educational Digest*, November, 1976: 39–42.

Chapter Four

Education According to Old Curriculum and its Impact on Modern Times

H. M. 'Abd Al-Quddus Qasmi'

Hafiz Muhammad Abdul Quddus Qasmi, a Pakistani, was born in 1914. He is Honorary Professor, University of Peshawar, Peshawar, Pakistan; a Member of the Board of Governors, Islamic Research Institute, Islamabad; formerly Head of Department of Islamiyat, University of Peshawar (1960–1974). He worked in Islamia College, Peshawar (1947–1960); Darul Uloom, Amritsar (1943–47); Oriental College, Srinagar (1941–43); Oriental College, Lahore (1939–1940). His publications include: critical editions of Ibn-ul-Fuwati's *Majmaul-Adab* (Vol. V) and of Bayazid Ansari's *Khairul Bayan*; Urdu translation of *Al-Urwatul Wuthqa*; articles in Urdu *Encyclopaedia of Islam* on Sunnah, Contents of the Holy Quran etc; text-books of Islamic Studies for schools and colleges.

I. Introduction

Before touching upon the actual subject I consider it appropriate to deal briefly with the history of Islamic studies in the early centuries of Islam. The sciences that kept the Muslims occupied since the very beginning of their history sprang from the Book of Allah, the Quran. So the Holy Book was the fountain of their views and thoughts. They read it, listened to it, and took great interest in its text and style. They arranged discussions around the meaning of its words. They thought over its different meanings. They learned it and taught its various chapters as a text.

Hence, the first of the studies that the Muslims brought into circulation was *'Ilm al-Tafsir* —the science of the exegesis of the Holy Quran. At first the task of interpretation of the words of the Holy Book was undertaken; then was added explanations based on traditions.

Muslims searched in the Quran and the traditions of the Holy Prophet Muhammad (Sunnah) (peace be on him) to solve most problems dealing with their religion. The study of Quran and Sunnah, the two main sources of the religion, were expanded in the coming centuries to include: reciting the Holy Quran, religious philosophy, diacritical marks, jurisprudence and its principles, the science of the exegesis of the Holy Quran, and studies of the traditions of the Holy Prophet, studies of the life history of the Prophet, and Islamic history.

Muslims relied in these sciences mostly on that which was narrated to them by the Holy Prophet and his Companions. They did not turn to independent opinions except when there remained no alternative.

As such, they categorized the entire available corpus of expressions of the scholars into: *al-Ilm* and *al-Ra'y*, so that the legists who tried to make necessary adjustments among different traditions were named as *As'hab al-Ra'y*, (the people of opinions), like al-Imam Abu Hanifa, al-Iman Malik, and all those who followed in their foot-steps.

But when Muslim scholars intermingled with non-Muslim scholars and with those who were newly converted into Islam, and the doors of discussion, debate, and difference of opinion were opened, Muslim scholars had to devise new arguments in order to clarify misunderstandings of non-Muslims, those misled or gone astray, as well as those who were influenced by their views. Thus the science of *Kalam* — and the class of *Mutakallimin* — emerged.

Late in the first century of Islam, Muslims came in contact with Greek sciences through translations. The first science to attract them was chemistry. Khalid ibn Yazid was the first who acquainted himself with this branch of knowledge —then others followed his suit in other areas of study. Thus treatises in metaphysics, theology, physics, and logic were translated.

Some of the views expressed in these treatises were contrary to the views put forward by Islamic *Shari'at*, hitting directly at the Islamic faith. It resulted in the division of Muslims into various groups. One group took all the claims of these scientists for granted and termed their sciences as classics, thus doubting the Islamic faith. This group thus became unbelievers and hypocrites.

Another group agreed with the first group in fundamentals, but did not take issue with it. So they interpreted the basic principles, trying to make necessary adjustments between the new philosophy and Islam. They are called the Muslim philosophers. There were others who defended Islamic beliefs in the light of their reason. If their reason did not accept any principles of Sunnah, they disapproved of them. They were called *Mu'tazila*.

In contrast to the above groups, a large group held fast to the book of Allah and Sunnah of the Holy Prophet. They rejected all that contradicted the two and worked hard to strengthen their defence against swindlers, with the help of rational and traditional arguments. They even considered it sufficient to say: 'We believe in what Allah has revealed; and that Allah knows and people know not.' Among them *Ahl al-Hadith, Ash'arites*, and *Maturidites* were called *Ahl al-Sunnah wa-al-Jama' at*.

The field of discussion and debate between Ash'arites and Mu'tazilites, centred around the misunderstanding of the Rationalists and the preservation of the basic faith, as has been described literally in the Book and in the Sunnah.

As for the philosophers, they were not touched by the scholastic theologians till Imam Ghazzali appeared on the scene. It was Ghazzali who gave in detail the sayings of the philosophers in his book, *Maqasidal-Falasifah*. Then in his other book —*Tahafut al-Falasifah*, he refuted those sayings of the philosophers which were not approved of by *the Shari'at*.[1]

It is pertinent to mention that Imam Ghazzali attempted to refute philosophers' views with his books and treatises.

Among his followers in this was Imam al-Razi. Yet there were some scholars who defended the passions of the philosphers after having made some minor readjustments. As a result, one may find in institutions which are run on old lines in the Indo-Pak sub-continent, those who study the books of Ibn Sina and his followers with the promise that they will read these arguments and reply to them later on (which never happens).

II. Arab and Ghaznavite Dynasties in Sindh

Religious studies in India have been in vogue since ancient times. In the 2nd, 3rd, and 4th centuries A.H. there were Arab dynasties in Sindh, under whose auspices the Arabic language spread in many cities, as is apparent from the stone tablets excavated from the remnants of the old cities, like Daibal and Bhamboor near Karachi. Al-Istakhri, Ibn Hawqal and al-Maqdisi relate to us that the residents of the bazaars in Mansoora, Daibul and Multan used to speak two languages —Arabic and Sindhi.[2]

Mumtaz Ahmad Pathan says that religious literature has played an important role in the development and diffusion of Arabic literature in Sindh. So there were written in Arabic, books on curricula as well as books on the exegesis of the Holy Quran and explanation of *Hadith*.

Mosques were the centres of teaching throughout Sindh, the famous among them being the religious centres at Mansoora, Daibal and Qusdar[3] (The present Khuzdar). Recently many articles and books have been written on the introduction of religious studies in Sindh in the beginning of the Islamic era, as well as on those who were educated in these institutions. Famous among these is *Rijal al-Sind wa-al Hind* by Qadi Athar Mubarakpuri.

As for the North of the Sub-Continent, especially the northern part of Pakistan, although Islam came here in the first three centuries, no records could be found —written or inscribed —of the first two centuries. Nevertheless, an epigraph, which is the oldest found in Arabic in the Sub-Continent, was found in Waziristan, within the territory of Pakistan. It was written in 143 A.H.[4] Except for that epigraph, there are no other details of the early occupation by Muslims of the northern area.

The historical details about Muslim states in the north of India begin with the Ghaznavites in general and with Muhammad of Ghaznah in particular. He invaded India a number of times (not less than twenty times), and succeeded in attaching Punjab to his Kingdom of Ghaznah, his viceregent being posted in Lahore, the Capital of the Punjab.

Mahmud of Ghazna was a religious King who can be counted among *Ahl al-Sunna*. He followed the Hanifi school of Fiqh and respected '*Ulama*' and pious people greatly. When he became the ruler of India, he wished the '*Ulama*' to visit India and make it the centre of religious activities. The result was that Lahore in the fifth century, and afterwards, became a cultural centre for scholars, preachers and mystics, flocking to it from Iran and neighbouring areas for spreading knowledge and preaching Islamic tenets.

Religious literature in this area was bilingual. Courses and scholarly books were written in Arabic, while books in Persian were written for general readers. However, the Persian language of those days was full of Arabic words, proverbs and selected sentences from the *Quran* and *Sunnah*. Thus the Persian language influenced the Arabic language. Thus the Arabic language in which books were composed in this era was not as lucid as that of Sindh in bygone centuries.

66

Whatever the state of the Arabic language, Arabic and Persian religious literature flourished, and the number of '*Ulama*' who spread religious knowledge increased. The most famous among them was al-Shaykh Ismail al-Lahori (d. 448/1052), who, it is said, was the first to introduce *al-Tafsir* and *Hadith* in the sub-continent. As for the curriculum of education in the times of the Ghaznavites, we know little about it.

III. Delhi Kings

Ghaznavi Dynasty in the sub-continent was confined to the Punjab alone. Then Ghawrides invaded India and expanded the Islamic state to the spacious plain in the North. The Ghawride Slave Dynasty succeeded Ghawrides, the most famous among them being Qutbud Bin Aibak who started the construction of a famous mosque in Delhi named Quwwat al-Islam. He constructed in it as a high minaret for the call to prayer which survived with all its grandeur, and remains a monument for national and international visitors and tourists. It is considered as one of the wonders of India.

Knowledge in this era was spread under the auspices of the Indian Kings, rulers, scholars and mystics. Thus there were schools and centres of knowledge in all the famous cities like Delhi, Lahore, Multan, Uch, Ajodhan, Nager, Ajmir, Badayun, Jaunpur, etc.

In this era the curriculum of education was identical with that of Iraq, Syria, Iran and Khurasan. In the vicinity of every mosque, there was a primary school where small children would learn and recite the Holy Quran, as well as the art of writing and Arabic grammar. One of the signs of Ulamas' great respect for the Holy Quran was that they taught the children writing, only with the help of proverbs and couplets. They revered the Holy Quran so much that they did not want to make it a drill ground for training children in Arabic writing. They used to teach writing with the help of wooden tablets which the children used to write on, then cleaned by washing when they no longer needed them.[5] Along with these institutions there were institutions for religious education, scattered throughout the country, though they had not been given particular names.[6]

The curriculum for these institutions was divided into two parts: Elementary, which was called *Nisab daruri* (compulsory curriculum);

and Higher, which was called *Nisab-i-fadila* (curriculum for specialization). However, we are unable to trace details of these curricula, and the syllabi that were in use in them; except that we can infer from the biographies of the scholars that the compulsory curriculum consisted of the reading of the Holy Quran, the teaching of the essential problems of belief and worship, and the teaching of some necessary lessons of Arabic and Persian literature, grammar, mathematics and algebra. It qualified the student for service in the administration. In the upper classes was taught al-Kafiyah of Ibn Hajib; al-Mufassal of al-Zamakh-shari in grammar; al-Mukhtasar of al-Qudusi; and Majma al Bahrayn of Ibn al-Sa'ati; in Fiqh al-Hanafi. We have been unable to trace further details in this connection.

The office bearers of the government were of two types: on the lower level, there were clerks in the office, and, on the higher level, there were officers, administrators, teachers, judges, Khatteebs, preachers and accountants. All of them used to take this curriculum first and then select for themselves courses suitable for their special branch of service. However, practical training with a teacher was the most important. Curriculum of the higher standard consisted of: *al-Kashshaf* of al-Zamakhshari, *al-Hidaya* of al-Murghinani, *Kanz al-Wusul* of al-Qadi al Bazdavi, *Mashariq al-Anwar* of al-Saghani, and *Masabin al-Sunnah* of al-Baghawi, and the like. Most were authentic and voluminous books. Many years were spent in studying these books in order to acquire fuller command of their words and contents.[7]

I think the curriculum in use in logic and philosophy was not associated with this curriculum. However, there were experts in these branches and whoever desired to study them used to turn to those scholars (cf. al Nazhat, 3: 104, 125, 146). The course in logic was *Resalat-al-Shamsiyyat* of Najmud Din Umar Ibn 'Ali al Qazwini (d. 693/1294); and *Kalam al-Sahaif* of Shamsud Din Muhammad Ibn Ashraf al-Husaini al-Samarkandi (d. 600–df.) Prescribed in the curriculum of education were books of character building and mysticism, like *al-Awarif* of al-Suhrawardi.

Students took a great interest in memorizing the Holy Quran and no specific age was fixed for this training. Rather there were Huffaz (people who had memorized the book of Allah by heart), and students gathered together around them and committed the Holy Quran to memory, whatever their age. The special feature of all this was the interest in religious training. Whenever a teacher disliked the manners

68

of a student (even in small matters of speaking), he refused to educate him further until he mended his ways.

Education and book-writing were influenced by the current literary taste. Thus books on usul al-Fiqh and ilmal-Kalam took on a philosophical colour, leaving no alternative for a great scholar other than turning to books on logic and philosophy. As such, *Ulama* in Delhi and their students flocked around '*al-Shamsiyyah*' and *Al-Saha'if*. But the rational sciences (like logic, scholastic study and philosophy) advanced well in the neighbouring countries of Iran and Iraq. Therefore, *Ulama* in Delhi felt a kind of vacuum in these Sciences in contrast to the position in other cities. This vacuum was filled by al-Shaykh al-Tulunbi. He migrated from Multan to Delhi, and started giving lessons in the rational sciences. Great titles were bestowed upon al Shaiykh al-Tulunbi, for one of the historians has described him as the crown of the '*Ulama*, Lamp of Excellence, unrivalled in his time in rational and traditional science, and matchless in his era in fundamentals and derivatives.

The gist of what is mentioned above of the history of sciences till the middle of 10th Century A.H. is that curriculum in education consisted of 'ilm al-Tafsir, al-Hadith, Fiqh, usul al-Fiqh, grammar and rhetoric on the one hand and scholastic theology, logic and philosophy on the other, along with Arabic and Persian literature and mathematics.

IV. Mughal Rule —Akbar's Period

The Mughal Emperor, Babur, conquered this part of the world in the 2nd quarter of the 10th Century A.H. after the Ludhis lost their power. It took a quarter of a century to strengthen the foundations of the new state, and for the pressure of Afghan revolts here and there to subside. The curriculum of education in the cities followed the same lines as that of the 9th Century. After the rule was fully established rational sciences began to appear and the '*Ulama*' from Iran came to these cities, taking great care of these sciences. Thus Nahw, rhetoric, usul al-Kalam and al-Tafsir took on a rational aspect. The evolution of sciences meant study of the text of the book, then its commentary, then marginal notes on the explanation, and marginal notes on marginal notes. For instance al-'Aqaid of al-Nasafi was commented upon by al-Taftazani, which was then commented upon by al-Khiyali, (and it was in a later period commented upon by al-Sialkoti); all these books were included in the curriculum in *al-Madaris al-Nizamiyyah*.

Centres of education increased in different capitals, like Delhi, Lahore, Multan, Jaunpur, Akbarabad, Ahmadabad, Burhanpur, Thalar, Kashmir, Mangarkot, and in famous towns like Amrohah, Sahswab, Saubral Sarhin, Ahamad Nagar, Bilgram, Narnol, Nagur, Bayanah, Jundiri, Gulbargah, Gilkandah, Bedar, Manakpur, Manir, Mandsur Radavli, Saharanpur and Khayraabad. In all these centres there were seminaris, and the reputation of a seminari depended on the reputation of the scholar who taught there. India of those days was crowned with *Ulama*-teachers —writers, judges, Deans, preachers, and mystic-teachers —around whom flocked students and public, Muslims and non-Muslims.

Side by side with these institutions were elementary schools in which was taught an essential syllabus which consisted of reading of the holy Quran, calligraphy, mathematics, and letter-writing in Persian. The students who qualified were employed in government offices. Muslims and non-Muslims alike used to read in these schools.

Books prescribed in the curriculum of these religious institutions were as follows:

Arabic Grammar: *Mizan al-Sarf* by al-Jurjani; *Lubbul-Albab* by al-Baydawi, *al-Irshad* by Dawlatabadi; and *Sharh-i-Kafia of Ibn Hajib* by al-Jami.

Fiqh: *Kanzal-Daqa'iq* by al-Nasafi; *Sharh Wiqayat al Riwaya* by Sadr al-Shari'ah: *Al-Hidayah* by al-Murghinani.

Usul al-Fiqh: *al-Mukhtasar* by Husami, *al-Manar* by al-Nasafi *Kashf al–Asrar* by al-Baydawi, *al-Tahwid* by al-Taftazani (a commentary on al-Tawhid by Sadr al-Shari 'at).

al-Kalam: *Sharh 'Aqaid al-Nasafi* by Taftazani, *al-Adudiyyah* by al-iji– and its commentary by al-Jurjani, and *Sharh al-Mawaqif* by the latter.

al-Balaghah: *al-Talkhis* by al-Khatib al-Sherbini; and its two commentaries —*al-Mukhtasar* and *al-Mutawal* by Taftazani; *Sharh al-Miftah* by Taftazani.

Al-Mantiq: *Sharh al-Shamsiyyat* by al-Razi; *al-Tahzib* by al-Taftazani; and its commentary by al-Yazdi and marginal notes by al–Pawwari; *Sharh Matali al-Anwar* by al-Razi: and its marginal notes by al-Jurjani.

'ilm al-Falah: *Bist Bab* (20 chapters) Ma'rif al-usturlab and Sharh
   al-Jughmini
Al-Geometry: *Tahrir-Uqlidas*
Al-Munazarah: *al-Risalat al-Sharif*
Al-Hadith: (which was taught at an advanced age)
   al-Arba'un by al-Nawawi
   Mishkat al-Masabih
   al-Shama'il by al-Tirmidhi
   al-Jami al-Shih of al-Bukhari,
   al-Shifa' by Qadi Ayad; and in some schools
   al-Sirah al-Sittah (the six authentic books)
Al-Tafsir: *Anwar al-Tanzil* by al-Baydawi
   al-Madarik by al-Nasafi.

V. Mughal Rule from Jehangir to Aurangzeb

In this period Arabic schools were the same as those in the 1st Mughal
period. However, compulsory education which applied to Muslims
and non-Muslims alike relied heavily on Persian books. And as the
Persian language contained many Arabic words, idioms and proverbs,
experts in this curriculum were quite capable of writing in Persian,
and, with the help of Persian, were well acquainted with Arabic.

Religious education schools increased in number day by day, till
they reached their zenith in the times of Aurangzeb, the learned, the
pious and the *Faqih*. This king spent liberally on the students and
granted lands to the teachers and the schools. Contacts between
'Ulama' of India and *'Ulama'* of Iran decreased. The Indian *'Ulama'*
thus concentrated on the rational and traditional sciences which they
had already studied in books, while adding to them explanations and
marginal notes of their own which were taught to the students.
Therefore, we see in this era *Sharh al-Manar* in Usul al-Fiqh of Sheikh
Ahmad, teacher of Aurangzeb, *Sullam al-'Ulum* in logic of Muhibullah
al-Bihari, and his *Musallam al-thubat* in usul al-Fiqh, *Hashiyah* of
Qadi Mirzahid al-Harawi on *al-Risalat al-Qutbiyyah Sharh al-Maybadhi
on Hidyat al-Hikmat* along with *Sharh al-Sadr* al Shirazi, *Al-Shams al-
Bazighah* of al-Jusjusi, *al Mirqat* of Fadl Imam al-Khayrabadi, and *al-
Hadyat al-Sa'idiyyah* of Abdul Haqq al-khayrabadi. All were included
in the syllabus.

Most unusual was the dedication of teachers and writers to *Sullam al-'Ulum* of Muhibullah al-Bihari. Many commentaries were written on this work including these of al-Mulla Mubeen, al-Mula Hasan, 'Abdul 'Ali Bahrul 'Ulum, Hamdullah al-Sindelavi, and al-Qadi Mubarak al-Kofamwe. All of these books were taught in religious institutions which became over-loaded with this type of discussion, leaving little time for other religious studies.

The predominant curriculum in the traditional seminaris was known as al-Dars al-Nizami. And it is said that this curriculum is attributed to al-Shaykh Nizamud Din al-Sihali. His father, Qutbud Din al-Sihali, was a great scholar, who evolved for his pupils a curriculum consisting of one book of moderate size in each field. Then his son Nizamud Din al-Sihali added to it one more book in each field. Thus two books were read in each of the fields. Al-Shaykh Nizamud Din al-Sihali had migrated to Luchnow, India. His descendants were known as '*Ulama*' Firangi Mahalli, Lucknow, and they had considerable influence. The most well-known among them in the last century was Maulana 'Abdul Hayy al-Lucknawi, whose books were edited by Professor 'Abdul Fattah Abu Ghaddah and are published in a befitting form.

However, the curriculum was not confined to the books prescribed by Nizamud Din al-Sihali. The '*Ulama*' later on added works of their own interests. Nevertheless, this curriculum lacked books in Ahadith. By the grace of Allah it happened that one of the most learned scholars of the sub-continent visited —in the manner prevalent in those days — the House of Allah and returned with a store of scholarship and new ideas which brought about revolution in Indian scholarship. This scholar was al-Shah Waliullah al-Dehlavi who made a pilgrimage to Mecca in the middle of 12th century A.H. He became the pupil of Abu Tahir al-kurdi al-Madani and then returned to India. He infused in the people love of the studies of the Quran, Ahadith and philosophy of religion. Thus Indian '*Ulama*' were introduced to the studies of Ahadith, especially *Mu'atta* of Imam Malik in addition to the Al-Sihah books which were in use earlier. In this way the old curriculum proceeded up to the Mughal period in the 13th century A.H.

The gist of what we have said in connection with the curriculum of education practised up to the middle of the last century is that religious seminaris had one and the same curriculum. In these seminaris were read books on Arabic grammar, Fiqh, and usul al-Fiqh, Arabic Literature, scholastic Theology, Logic, Philosophy with its different kinds, Hadith and Tafsir. Side by side with these seminaris were elementary schools where children learnt to read the Holy Quran, and were taught the Persian Language and letter writing. This enabled them to work in the offices of the government. And there were schools for memorizing the Holy Quran and the art of reciting it. Arabic and Persian languages were so dominant in the government offices and literary circles that all Indians, Muslims and Hindus, were taught one culture. In their private conversations they used proverbs in Persian as well as Persian verses from the classics of Persian literature. Hindu scholars, when writing books started them in the name —and praise — of Allah and gave blessings to the Prophet.

Thus the curriculum was divided into:

(1) general, in which Muslims and non-Muslims alike were participants, (2) special, exclusively for Muslim scholars, and (3) special, exclusively devoted to old Hindu studies. Yet Islamic studies were prevalent above all other studies and were high cultural ideals. The government used to grant Muslim scholars scholarships, allowances and pieces of land. Likewise there were scholars who relied on their private resources to carry on with the service of knowledge for the sake of Allah.

VI. The Period of English Occupation

After the English had obtained full control of the Indian subcontinent in the middle of the last century, they devised a new curriculum of education. As for the old curriculum, they, at the beginning, established new schools in which they changed the old curriculum while adding things important to them and excluding things important to Muslims. For instance, in Lahore they established an oriental college for which the following curriculum in advanced classes was prescribed:

1. al-Balaghah: *Sharh al-Talkhis al-Mutawal* by al-Taftazani.
2. al-Adab al-Arabi: *al-Maqame, Diwan al-Hamasah, Diwan al-Mutanabbi, 'Arub al-Miftah.*
3. Logic, philosophy and dialecticism:
   Sharh al-Sullam by Hamidullah; and *Sharh* by Qadi Mubarak; *al-Risalat al-Rashidiyyah, Sharh Hidayat al-Hikmat* by al-Sadr al-Shirazi.

4. al-Fiqh: *al-Hidayat* by al-Marghinani, adding to it an explanation of some points from other reliable sources.
5. Ilm al-Tafsir and Hadith were not taught here, though after noting Muslim interest in them, the English included them in the curriculum.

Muslims were not satisfied with the schools established by the English. They set up their own local institutions for the teaching of Islamic studies where the curriculum was the same as in the institutions of the last days of the Mughal empire. The most famous of these institutions was Dar al-'Ulum of Deoband which became and is still known throughout the Muslim world. Students from the far-flung areas of India, Afghanistan, Qazan, Turkistan, Java, Malaya and Ceylon came to it. Deoband Seminari became so famous in India that it was called Azher al-Hind. Side by side with it were other small and big institutions, like Mazahir al-'Ulum Saharanpur, and Madrasah Firangi Mahal of Lucknow, and the like.

However, a majority of the inhabitants of the sub-continent accepted the new curriculum of education as it assisted them in obtaining their livelihood through joining the government service. The foreign rulers adopted the policy of divide and rule, which favoured the Hindus, a policy which created in Muslims a sense of competition. This led the latter to rush to acquire education under the new curriculum, in order to get their share of the government service.

Muslims were divided into two groups: the first group readily accepted the new system of education enabled its members to acquaint themselves with the new culture, secure employment, and learn modern sciences which were most important in establishing the state under the new prevailing system. This new curriculum was enforced under the auspices of a secular system, in which religion and its teachings had no place. Thus the generation which was brought up and taught under this system was unaware of the fundamentals of its religion. Nothing was as important to it as the means of subsistence, food, clothes, wealth and status. It knew much about the affairs of this world but was quite negligent of the Hereafter. Some of the scholars learnt of the Western views and penetrated deep in apostasy and unbelief. Others used to interpret the Nusus in the same way as the Muslim philosophers used to do in early centuries. Another group, holding fast to the old curriculum, preserved, under foreign domination, traditional integrity and fundamentals of Din as best as they could.

They generally preferred life in the Hereafter to life in this world. Their main emphases were on studies of the Quran, Sunnah, and Fiqh and the traditional studies, which they called auxiliary studies. Their character in this was like the character of their predecessors from Ahl-al-Sunnah. Nevertheless, by persevering and holding fast to the old system, they remained aloof from the modern sciences which were changing the old conceptions completely.

For instance, they taught in their books that the moon is in the first sky, the sun in the fourth, and the stars in the eighth (and it is *al-Kursi* in the term of Shariah). These eight skies are surrounded by a ninth one, which in Shariah's term is 'Arsh. And all the skies revolve round the earth, which is stationary. It was the thousand-years-old concept of Ptolemi; and it is the concept of those '*Ulama*' who read under the old curriculum in this modern age of ours.

Thus two schools of thought evolved, each one being happy with what it was doing; but the first group accused the second of being ignorant of modern sciences; while the second accused the first of being ignorant of Din, accusing it also of apostasy.

People then realized defects in both these curricula, and called for moderation in both of them, by including traditional science in the new curriculum and modern science in the old one. This idea was initiated by the ruler of the State of Hyderabad, where Din was a compulsory subject in all stages of education. So a department related particularly to Din was set up. The new system consisted of: English, the Arabic language, Fiqh and its principles, Tafsir, and Hadith. This moderation in the curriculum succeeded to some extent through the efforts of the scholars whom the government had appointed for the purpose.

Likewise in Aligarh University, the authorities concerned included religious studies in the curriculum, establishing a department where Din was taught, and successful candidates were awarded the B.A. Degree in religion. Honestly speaking, these efforts yielded very little fruit as candidates did not receive much religious instruction in these Universities.

They however, familiarized themselves with the name of Islam and loved it. This love infused in them the spirit of Jihad in the path of freedom and the establishment of an independent Muslim state — Pakistan—may Allah protect it from evils, calamities, straying and loss.

Criticizing the old curriculum, some said: it is useless, and needs replacing but others said: it is useful up to a point, but needs reshaping. The well known scholar, Shibli al-Nu'mani, was one of those who supported the second opinion. He wrote many articles criticizing the old education curriculum e.g.

1. Most books prescribed for the old curriculum consisted of discussions with no relation whatsoever to the subject matter. A student wasted his time in learning useless material;

2. In many of the books of the old curriculum sciences were taught as one, which confused a student who could not differentiate one from the other. For instance, Sullam al-'Ulam is a book in logic, prescribed in the old curriculum for reading along with its commentaries. These commentaries were over-burdened with talk about theology which was related to the study of philosophy.

3. The old curriculum made auxiliary subjects its main goal and contained many of these subjects. The main studies of religion, and particularly the Tafsir, were quite neglected.

4. There were in the old curriculum, many books on grammar; but these were not useful to the student as students who read these books were unable to write even a single line of Arabic.

5. There were certain principles in modern science which attacked Din-il Islam, and it was essential to refute them. However, there is nothing in the old curriculum which enabled a student to make an adequate reply.

This criticism was ignored by supporters of the old curriculum. They stated that any change in the curriculum created difficulties for institutions. On the other hand this very old curriculum did succeed with the graduation of some extraordinary scholars like Qasim Nanotwi.

But change and moderation were necessary and this challenge was accepted by some of the great scholars who established a society named Nadwat al-'Ulama, and an institution named Darul 'Ulum Nadwat al-'Ulama. The curriculum devised included books on traditional science as well as on Arabic Literature by early Muslim scholars. It also included works on English language and history. Some administrators of al-Nadwat interpreted the Nusus in a way that was not liked by the old 'Ulama'. Hence, upholders of the old curriculum identified those administrators with Mu'tazilah. However, in the second half of the twentieth century the Nadwah adopted a system flavoured with religion and piety, by the sincere efforts of pious scholars like al-Sayyed Sulaiman al-Nadwi and al-Shaykh 'Abu al-Hasan 'Ali al-Nadwi.

Briefly the education curriculum during English domination, was divided into three categories:

First, the new curriculum offered by government Universities and by Universities set up under the auspices of the government in power, like Aligarh University. This had no allowance worthy of the name for religious education, and its graduates were not well versed in religion.

Second, an old curriculum in use in Deoband under the auspices of the great 'Ulama' like Muhammad Qasim Nanotwi, al-Shaykh Mahmud Hasan, al-Shaykh Anwar Shah, al-Shaykh Husain Ahmad and al-Shaykh Shabbir Ahmad, which was more active to protect Din and preserve its fundamentals and rules. That is why some English people were surprised to see Indian Muslims holding so fast to their religion. This was the result of incessant efforts by Darul 'Ulum of Deoband and other institutions in this connection.

Third, the curriculum in practice in Nadwat al-Ulama' succeeded in producing scholars and writers capable of writing books in accordance with modern requirements, books which could satisfy the enquiring minds of modern scholars. The most famous of these writers was al-Sayyed Sulaiman al-Nadwi, and Professor Abul Hasan Ali al-Nadwi.

VII. The Old Curriculum after the Establishment of the Islamic State of Pakistan

When Pakistan came into being in 1947, the slogan of the founding party was the Kalimah (There is no God but Allah). It meant to show that Pakistan came into being in order to make the word of Allah operative. And as none of the most famous institutions was in Pakistan, the Pakistanis desired to found some of their own. Thus the State established universities, a school system, and colleges with modern educational curricula, and added to them instruction in religion at all levels (elementary, secondary, and post graduate). Religious instruction was made a compulsory subject in some stages and elective in others. In every University was established a highly qualified department of Islamic studies. Graduates were appointed as lecturers in the colleges and the instruction is far better now than it was during the rule of the English.

Institutions with the old curriculum on the pattern of Deoband were set up by scholars in every city and estimated, in all, to total 900. The most famous are the Darul'Ulum at Karachi, run under the auspices of the (late) Mufti Muhammad Shafi; al-Madrasah al-'Arabiyyah at Karachi, under the guidance of al-Shaykh Muhammad Yusuf al-Banori; and al-Jami'ah al-Ashrafiyyah at Lahore, which is run under the supervision of the sons of the late Mufti Muhammad Hasan. Some of these institutions follow the old curriculum to the letter, while some others allow very minor changes.

The government and the people tried their level best to create institutions offering a moderate curriculum of education and an Islamic University at Bahawalpur and a Theology Madrasah at Peshawar came into being. It is expected that the government of Kashmir will establish at Mirpur a third institution on this pattern.

I was a teacher, and member of the Board of Studies of the Theology Madrasah, for 25 years since its establishment in 1949, and chairman for the last 15 years, also a member of the Committees of courses in the other two for the University of Peshawar. Here there are separate colleges for the teaching of Engineering and Medicine, and separate departments for teaching literature, arts and sciences—all these being affiliated to the Universities. In the same way there will be a department for the teaching of religious studies, also affiliated to the University. The conditions for admission into this department will be the same as those of other departments. Only those students who have passed the secondary school certificate examination will be admitted. The four years course of the college will qualify the student for appearing for the Bachelor of Theology Examination of the University of Peshawar and successful candidates will be awarded B.Th. Degree of the University.

Courses will consist of English, Urdu, Arabic, History, Tafsir Hadith, Fiqh and the principles of these last three. Extra-curricular activities will be the same as are prescribed for the other students of secular subjects. After the degree course there will be an opportunity for the post-graduate degree of M.A. for which a two year course is prescribed. A student will read al-Tafsir, al-Hadith, Usul Al-Din, al-Fiqh, comparative studies of religion, history, Philosophy of Religions and essay writing.

The curriculum of education of Bahawalpur University is devised in such a way that a student must be competent in religious studies, Arabic Literature, along with some other secular sciences, old and new. And for the sciences some compulsory topics have been included in the curriculum along with some other elective ones. The second combination of political science, history, economics, and Arabic literature, a student has the option of taking any two subjects. There are also courses for specialization in al-Tafsir, al-Hadith, al-Fiqh and Arabic literature and a college for the training of preaching.

VIII. Concluding Remarks

It is apparent that Islamic studies means the Holy Quran, the art of reciting it, and its exegesis, Ahadith, their reading, and understanding, and deducing rules of law from them, i.e. al-Fiqh and al-Ijtihad. To be accomplished in these studies a student must have full command of Arabic grammar and Ussul al-Fiqh and Ahadith.

Thus a scholar must have the capability of responding to any misunderstanding, old or new, created about Islamic beliefs. He must have training in academic theology, and be capable of putting forward rational arguments to support the fundamentals of Din. But for the removing of the misundertandings created by the old Greek philosophy or modern European sciences (including politics, sociology, economics, and philosophy) it is essential that the scholar must be completely familiar with them, so that he may compare them with Islamic studies and detect their mistakes. There is no alternative for a Muslim scholar if he is to be aware of new ideas in politics, economics, sociology, geography, and in the studies of philosophy, science, medicine and technology.

A student of Islamic studies also needs command over any language he wants to use, the most important being Arabic and English, and any language which would be needed for teaching Islam in Eastern and Western cities. Likewise he might need to read books on Islam written in foreign languages in order to appreciate what has been written.

It is impossible for a single individual to have command of all these subjects as Islam needs:

1. Scholars to teach in the secondary schools.
2. Scholars specialized in all branches of Islamic studies, for conducting seminars in colleges of religious studies or in religious schools.
3. Scholars and legists capable of evolving rules for new problems.
4. Research scholars to resolve problems of modern times.
5. Scholar-preachers who could give religious talks, and encourage good and forbid evil in mosques and at social gatherings.
6. Scholars capable of producing scholarly literary articles, but writing at the same time useful material for the general public.
7. Missionary scholars, capable of diffusing Islam e.g. in Japan in Japanese; in Korea in Korean, in China in Chinese and in Africa in African-English-French language combinations. It is also essential that these missionaries should have some acquaintace with the religions of the people to whom they teach Islam; and that they should answer objections to Islam in a scholarly manner.
8. Preacher-scholars capable of resisting movements of a destructive nature and of removing successfully, misunderstandings. And these preachers must have full information on destructive factions. They must also have a specialization in one of these destructive forces.
9. We also need ladies of scholarly acumen to shoulder the responsibility of preaching and teaching ladies. There should be separate institutions for appropriate training.

These requirements —the establishment of different kinds of schools and universities —must be met, so that students can be coached in accordance with the rules prescribed for the purpose.

It is incumbent upon Muslims in general and Muslim leaders in particular to execute their duty with regard to the establishment of schools and universities of this type. Finally, I would like to add that although this article refers mainly to Pakistan, these requirements concern the entire Muslim world. Although they are partly fulfilled by al-Azhar University, Madinah, and other Universities in Saudi

Arabia, and Bahawalpur University at Bahawalpur, Pakistan, they need to be met on an international scale.

NOTES

1. An important statement of al-Ghazali is that engineering and mathematics are two optional sciences which can be acquired as far as we need them. Logic and theology are two branches of al-Kalam which can be acquired in a similar fashion. In theology philosophers follow different schools, some of which lead to apostasy and others to baseless innovation. In the studies of metaphysics, some lead to ignorance and must be avoided; others are permissible, and can be acquired. (Ihya' ulum al-Din, Kitab al–'Illm):
Ibn Khaldun states, 'These studies (studies in philosophy) are not very much needed in social matters; but are very harmful to Din. Those who are fed up with things of religious concern, give importance to them, and those who do not know even the A.B.C. of religious studies give no attention to them'. (6th Fasl, in First Book, Chapter 24)

2. Al-Istakh-ri, Ibn Hawqal, 326, al-Maqdisi, 479.

3. Mumtaz Ahmad Pathan's article on 'Arabic literature under Arab rule in Sind', reproduced in *History of Muslim literature in the Indo-Pak* Sub-Continent (in Urdu). Vol 2, 52.

4. This tablet has been preserved in Peshawar Museum. Its text is: 'It has been written at the order of Ibn Amman, May Allah accept his good deeds, and forgive his evil ones, and it was written on Friday the 13th of Jumad al-Ula, 243 A.H. blessings of Allah may be upon Muhammad and his followers'(*Journal of Oriental College*, Lahore, August, 1942).

5. Ihsan Ilahi Rana's article on 'Arabic literature under Delhi's Kingdom' produced in the '*History of Muslim Literature in the Indo-Pak Sub-Continent*, Vol. 2.

6. Except that he mentions in the biography of al-Qazi Minhajuddin Siraj in Ta'rikh-i-Tabqat-i-Nasri that he was a teacher in Fairoziyyah and Nisiriyyah Schools in Delhi.

7. See *Nazhat al-Khawater* by Abdul Hayy al-Hussaini, Vol. 2: 23, 28, 159. Abdul Muqtadar, Qasim Ibn Umar and Nasiruddin Mahmud.

Chapter Five

Islamic Education of Muslim Children in the West and the Problem of Curriculum and Syllabus

Afzalur Rahman

Afzalur Rahman (b. 1915) M.A. (Punjab). Was the founder of the U.K. Islamic Educational Trust and its Founder-Chairman since 1964. Taught in various colleges of the Punjab University between 1943 and 1955 and in the Schools of London County Council and Saudi Arabia between 1956 and 1964. Participated in the Muslim Organizations Conference held at Mecca in 1974 and the First International Islamic Conference held at Mecca in 1976. Publications include *Pakistan Economics and Ilm Muashiyat: (Economic Doctrines of Islam)*.

Main Problems

Muslims living in the West are facing, directly or indirectly, many problems regarding the religious education of their children. The following, with particular reference to the United Kingdom, are the main problems:

1. The Muslims are scattered all over the country and are divided into small pockets of population based on their affiliation to the country and even province of their origin.

2. They are not properly organized, or even rightly guided, to use their collective power to influence the central or local government to solve their cultural, educational or religious problems. Most Muslim parents in Britain are even ignorant of their legal and social rights regarding the religious education of their children.

3. Parents are busy earning their living and have very little time to pay attention to the religious education of their children.

4. A number of parents are so impressed by Western civilization

that they are quite happy with the present situation and have no desire to provide their children with religious education.

5. Practical difficulties of distance separating the scattered Muslim communities are another hazard in the way of organizing religious education.

6. There is a general lack of resources, a shortage of good books on Islam in the English language, and difficulty in obtaining both teachers who are really dedicated and are fully equipped—in character, knowledge and personality—and proper religious centres and schools.

7. There is the problem of finding single sex schools in Britain and other parts of Europe. Islam rejects the idea of the free mixing of members of the opposite sex and Muslims, therefore, want their children to receive education in single sex schools. This problem is becoming acute as the Labour Government has introduced comprehensive education in all areas of the U.K. Almost all single sex schools are being merged into mixed schools and are therefore, creating a problem for the Muslims of Britain.

8. Western society has almost become a multi-cultural and multi-religious society. The impact of different cultures and religions upon each other has never been so great as it is to-day. Muslim children in the West are living in such a society and therefore face grievous problems.

9. Secularism and agnosticism are becoming very popular philosophies in Western countries and many of the young people are becoming more and more irreligious.

10. Although the grip of the Christian religion on the State as well as on the people has weakened, missionary propaganda, to court young people of other religious minorities living in the country, has gained considerable force.

11. With the increase in wealth and material gain, morals and faith have been almost eroded and have given way to immorality and the fulfilment of sensual pleasures. Selfish desires have taken over moral values, and obscenity in literature, dress and social life is widespread. The whole of society is totally corrupt and has an adverse effect on children.

12. Even the concept of Christian religious education in schools has undergone a dramatic change for the worse and it is liable to affect adversely the attitude of Muslim children towards their own religion.

13. While Muslim parents are facing internal and external difficulties, their children are left to face a three-pronged onslaught of secularism, atheism and liberalism at home, in school, and from their surroundings and society.

14. Anti-Islamic forces are well organized in the West and are trying their best to present a distorted picture of Islam through local and international mass media, and this is likely to create a false impression in the minds of Muslim youth about their religion.

Meaning and Principles of Education

It is obvious that education cannot be neutral towards the culture and ideals of people as is advocated by the supporters of liberal education. If education is divorced from religion and moral values, it will lead to the disintegration and destruction of the social fabric of society. This may be seen from the achievements of liberal education in the West as well as in the East.

In the words of Walter Lippman, 'The schools and colleges have been sending out into the World, men who no longer understand the creative principles of society in which they must live. Deprived of their cultural tradition, the newly educated Western men no longer possess in the form and substance of their own minds and spirits, the ideas, premises, the rationale, the logic, the method, the values of Western civilization — the present education is destined, if it continues, to destroy Western civilization and is in fact destroying it'.[1]

Professor Harold H. Titmus writes, 'Even more serious than the lack of a common store of knowledge is the lack of common ideals and convictions. Education too frequently fails to build up any vital affirmations, convictions and discipline. There has been a dangerous separation of science and research from human values and loyalties — education has divorced itself from the spiritual heritage of the past but has failed to supply any adequate substitute. Consequently even educated persons are left without convictions of a sense of values as well as without a consistent World-view'.[2]

According to Mr. M. V. C. Jeffreys, 'The most serious weakness in modern education is the uncertainty about its aims. A glance over

84

history reminds us that the most vital and effective systems of education have envisaged their objectives quite definitely; in terms of personal qualities and social situations. In contrast Education in the liberal democracies is distressingly nebulous in its aims'.[3]

Western liberal education has totally failed to give any definite and precise objective or even to develop social ideas among students. It has failed to inspire the new generation with moral and cultural values. It deals merely with the needs of the body and fails to provide for the needs of the soul. Further, it has failed to organize knowledge into one consistent whole. In consequence, students see life and the world in small and unrelated parts and fail to understand their meaning and significance as a whole. Above all, modern liberal education has failed to produce men of understanding who fully grasp the fundamental issues of life.

These weaknesses of modern education are becoming increasingly manifest, and responsible persons in the West are beginning to recognize its drawbacks.

Dr. Albert G. Sims, Vice President, Institute of International Education, writes, 'The central problem in U.S. education to which all others are tangent is that of defining and giving effect to objectives and philosophy. It is no answer to say to this that the educational system mirrors in these respects the society which it serves. Education is also the means by which a community must deliberately project the image of its future'.[4]

The same idea is clearly put forward by the Rockefeller Reports on U.S. Education in these words, 'They (the students) want meaning in their lives. If their era, and their culture and their leaders do not or can not offer them great meanings, great objectives, great convictions, then they will settle for shallow and trivial meanings. People who live aimlessly, who allow the search for meaning in their lives to be satisfied by shady and meretricious experiences, have simply not been stirred up by any alternative meanings—religious meanings, ethical values, ideas or social and civic responsibility, high standards of self realization. This is a deficiency for which we all bear responsibility.'

'We must assume that education is a process that should be infused with meaning and purpose, that everyone will have deeply held beliefs, that every young man will wish to serve the values which have nurtured him and made possible his education and his freedom as an individual.'

And Sir Walter Moberly writes, 'Our predicament is this: Most students go through our universities without ever having been forced to exercise their minds on the issues which are really momentous. Under the influence of academic neutrality they are subtly conditioned to unthinking acquiescence in the social and political status quo and in a secularism on which they have never seriously reflected. Owing to the prevailing fragmentation of studies they are not challenged to decide responsibility on a life-purpose or equipped to make such a decision wisely. . . . Fundamentally they are uneducated.'[5]

Thus the experience of modern liberal education has clearly shown that the concept of neutrality in education is harmful to human values, culture and society and to its progress. Inevitably this concept causes society to move towards secularism and gradually, but surely, towards an irreligious and immoral life. It replaces all positive and moral values by material and immoral ways of life. And man becomes, in fact, a slave to his self and its desires.

Liberalism and Religious Education

Religious education in the West has also been greatly affected by Liberalism. As pointed out by the British Religious Education Council in a pamphlet entitled 'Religious Education in Primary Schools', 'Since the publication of "Learning for Life" there have been many important developments in the Primary curriculum, but none of them can be more exciting than those taking place in the field of religious education.

'In view of these developments, religious education is not to be regarded as a means of instructing young children in religious dogma, but rather as a way of helping them to face their disappointments and problems by presenting them with opportunities to explore their emotions, thus enhancing and developing their feelings of wonder, joy and awe.'

This booklet brings together a number of topics which can be developed in such ways. They explore the world of children's feelings and can be taken part of, or all the way, into a study of what is implicitly religious according to the need of the class and the desire of the teacher.

Many teachers of religious education do not believe in religious education because according to them, it is indoctrination and not open to critical study and leads to the point of view that it is impossible to find rational grounds for the continued inclusion of religious education in the curriculum.

Religious Education

Many modern teachers and others are of the opinion that religious education must be understood as a subject in which the great majority feel they can participate, and its presence in the curriculum should be justified on educational grounds alone. In many secondary schools it is called 'religious studies' and changes in thought and attitude towards religion are reflected in the C.S.E. and G.C.E. syllabuses.

Religious Studies

In practical terms, in other words in terms of the classroom, religious studies are about initiating children into an understanding of religion, (this is often called the phenomenological approach) and as such, they are concerned with two main areas of study, the implicit and the explicit.

The implicit is concerned with the main aspects of religion, with the problem of personal identity and with the meaning of life. In the case of young children religious education thus consists of sharing with them some of the religious feelings which have been the source of much inspiration in art, architecture, music, poetry and literature.

The following list of objectives of religious education point the way it is going in the United Kingdom and other Western countries:

1. to acknowledge the basic need for belonging, love and acceptance.
2. to help children to have an awareness of their needs and feelings and a sympathetic understanding of the needs and feelings of others.
3. to begin to understand quality in relationship, the demands and responsibilities they incur, and to make some progress in achieving such quality.
4. to create a situation for experiencing these relationships.

5. to help children explore the realms of mystery, wonder, awe and joy which are the basic emotions of religious experience.

Religious Education in a Multi-Cultural Society

As Britain and some of the other Western countries are becoming multi-cultural and multi-religious societies, the nature of religious education is undergoing yet a further dramatic change. Now a hotch-potch of all religions is taught in schools. It is thought that this provides a great opportunity for integrating children from different cultures into the life of the school.

The whole concept of religious education is changing and even the British Council of Churches is now saying that 'since the Local Education Authorities' school can no longer be expected to carry any more responsibility in principle for Christian nurture than for the nurture of Muslims, Jews or humanists, local churches must accept full responsibility for the Christian nurture of their young.' (The Child in the Church).

The Birmingham syllabus takes the view that the subject should be religious education, emphasizing both these words. Religions, a study of which continues to form the major part of the syllabus, are to be presented in order to increase understanding and to encourage personal growth and independent response to living, and are studied in the context of the secular ways of life.

This approach has also been supported by the Free Church Federal Council in the report, 'Religious Education in Church Schools'. The Free Church report accepts that the syllabus should include 'the ideological stands of those unable to accept or practise the tenets of any religious faith'. The more conservative Association of Christian Teachers (in 'Religious Education—a Considered View') agrees that there should be 'an examination of other significant world views' and these will include 'world views which have no overt religious basis.' It is quite explicit against the old belief and says that religious education 'does not try to produce in children a commitment to prescribed beliefs', and it talks instead of children making intelligent and personal commitments.

The discussion document produced by the Religious Education

Council concludes: 'Recommendations. 1. That the subject should be regarded as helping pupils to become educated about religions and other life stances and to be both appreciative and critical of them.' ('What Futute for the Agreed Syllabus?').

A very similar statement was issued by the Christian Education Movement (Education Guardian, March 23, 1976) which sees religious education as education which will help children to find their own beliefs.

The humanists go beyond this and insist that if religion is considered an integral part of education, then 'it must also be accepted that non-religious belief has a basic and integral place'. ('Objective, Fair and Balanced: a New Law for Education').

'Humanists believe that conduct should be based on humanity, insight and reason. People must face their problems with their own moral and intellectual resources, without looking for super-natural aid. Our concern is with this life, which we therefore strive to make worthwhile.' ('Humanist and Society—A General Statement of Policy', as revised by the 1976 HBM).

This liberal attitude towards religious education is being increasingly adopted in Western countries. The importance of new factors is stressed in a book entitled 'Discovering an Approach', MacMillan Education. It is the work of a Schools Council curriculum development project—'Religious Education in Primary Schools'. It emphasizes that any programme of religious education for children ought to take account of the ways in which a child comes to terms with his world. The programme must build upon his everyday experience and take note of the influence upon him of home and society. It should recognize that he is growing up as a member of a multi-faith society and find ways of helping him to appreciate the significance of religion (including a non-religious belief system).

Underlying the detailed suggestions is the idea that religious education should be characterized by openness, an exploratory attitude and the desire to foster understanding. Openness demands that religious education is not restricted to one particular tradition but takes seriously the existence in our society of different religions and secular alternatives to religious beliefs. It means that the scope of the subject and its content are not defined from within one particular religious tradition.

Exploration is the keynote both of the child's attempt to come to terms with his world and the place of religion within it, and of the teacher's efforts to help him. The child has begun a journey; his route ought not to be too exactly plotted. To emphasize the fostering of understanding is to place religious education within the educational pattern of the school. It directs the teacher's attention to the development of capacities and attitudes as well as to the imparting of knowledge.

It appreciates the importance of building religious education upon the child's growing awareness of himself, his relations with others and with the world around us.

Lastly, it begins the process of familiarizing children with religion, drawing upon their experience wherever possible and concentrating upon the exploration of activity rather than systems of belief.

Thus there seems to be a general trend of all opinions, including religious as well as secular, towards more liberalism in religious education leading almost to a non-religious or irreligious type of religious education in schools. This is happening in Britain, and other Western countries are not far behind. This type of religious education is trying to make children their own masters, liberating them from the bondage of belief—or the idea of God. Such religious education also gives new values to the young generation who do not recognize any absolute and permanent values.

Muslim Approach

The European brand of liberalism is hostile to religion and all that it stands for. The natural result of these changes is that the average Western youth who steps into practical life after completing his school education neither believes in any religion or moral values nor has any ideal to achieve in his life. His life is steered by his biological needs and sensuous desires. This type of education and the philosophy which prevails in educational institutions in the West is diametrically opposed to the Islamic philosophy of education. There is bound to be a dominant Christian element in multi-faith studies, and all other religions, including Islam, are taught by Christian or other non-Muslim teachers who do not, for obvious reasons, present the true picture of Islam. Gradually Muslim children will be integrated into Western society.

Many Muslim parents living in the West are worried about the religious education of their children and the influence of Christianity and Western culture in the schools. It is a cause of great concern for them as their children are exposed to non-Islamic influences at school. This fear of Muslim parents is pointed out by the British Community Relations Commission in its report entitled 'Religious Education in a multi-religious Society'. As religious education in schools is concerned almost exclusively with Christian doctrine and ethics, Muslim parents would like to withdraw their children from such classes.

Muslim children in the West are living in two conflicting cultures, one at home and the other school and in society. Lack of proper atmosphere and confused multi-cultural and multi-religious education at school and unrestricted liberty and permissiveness in society are very dominant factors which are likely to drive Muslim children away from Islamic principles and values. A very sound and balanced Islamic education is necessary to protect our young generation from the onslaught of Western influences and to keep them within the fold of Islam as practising Muslims.

The philosophy which dominates Western culture in general and Western education in particular, is not only diametrically opposed but also positively hostile to the Islamic philosophy of life. A Muslim youth finds himself in a society where his friends and others dance, drink and freely move in mixed gatherings with persons of their choice and have unrestricted sexual relationships before and after marriage, without having any regard for their parents, church or community. They are not bound by any moral and religious values or social norms. A Muslim youth lives in this type of atmosphere at school as well as outside the school.

Young Muslims are living in conditions totally unfavourable to Islamic ideals—the school, the surroundings and society at large are all corrupt and extremely hostile to Islamic education and learning: even the home where the child gets his first and basic education and training is not completely safe from Western influences, mainly through the mass media, and in particular T.V. and radio.

In view of these un-Islamic forces and unhealthy social and educational surroundings Muslim youth must be equipped with a sound Islamic education and trained to follow philosophy and appreciate Islamic culture. Only a genuine effort on the part of the Muslim community and a comprehensive system of education and training can protect the new Muslim generation living in the West from unhealthy trends and temptations.

There is no doubt that the majority of people are aware of the danger to which their children are exposed in Western society but they do not fully appreciate the severity and dimensions of the danger. Moreover, many of them are not fully equipped to provide the right education and training for their children to face this danger.

The Muslim communities in some areas of Britain have made arrangements for the religious education of their children in mosques, local county schools and community centres, in the form of evening and week-end classes, but these arrangements are not satisfactory and so very few children attend the classes. Moreover, these schools do not have the proper class-room atmosphere and necessary facilities, and therefore, fail to appeal to modern youth born and bred in the West. How far and in what way true Islamic education can be given to the new Muslim generation in the West, firstly to counter atheistic beliefs in the guise of liberalism and secondly to keep our youth on the path of the Islamic ideal, is a big problem awaiting a solution. It is high time that Muslims rose to the occasion and gave the problem top priority.

Purpose of Education

Education is not an end in itself but a means to an end. The end is to become something or achieve some objective. Most Western scholars agree that it is through education that a cultural and intellectual heritage is passed to the next generation. According to Dr. Iqbal, life of an individual depends on the body and soul. The life of a nation depends on the preservation of its traditions and culture. An individual dies if the life flow ceases. A nation dies if the ideals of its people are ignored.

Parents generally educate their children so that they may be able to secure a good job, but such education is only for the purpose of earning a living. Some regard the acquisition of knowledge to be the purpose of education, others consider the service of the community or the making of good citizens to be education's aim; but there are many people who put forward other ideas on this subject about which there is no common agreement.

The goal of education for a Muslim is to become an obedient and righteous servant of Allah. Education should turn the natural inclinations of students in the right direction and enable them mentally, physically, culturally, morally and practically to become grateful servants of Allah. They should be moulded through education so that they always think, plan, and act according to the Will of their Creator and Sovereign—Allah. This in Islam is the right, comprehensive and basic objective of education. Education must instil the beliefs and ideals for which Islam stands. It must also try to preserve and promote the culture and basic principles of Islam. Some Western scholars even realize and emphasize this aspect of education, e.g. A. N. Whitehead emphasized this point when he said that 'the essence of education is that it should be religious'.[6]

According to Dr. Iqbal, Islam should be the purpose of our life and education. He explained the meaning of *ilm* (knowledge) in a letter to one of his friends. He wrote, 'By *ilm* I mean that knowledge which is based on the senses. This knowledge yields physical powers which should be subject to *din* (i.e. religion of Islam). If it is not subject to *din* then it is evil, pure and simple. It is a duty of Muslims to Islamicize knowledge. Abu Lahab should be converted to Haider, or in other words, if it (knowledge) becomes subject to *din* then it will be a great blessing to mankind'.[7] Dr. Iqbal showed clearly that Islamic ideology was the purpose of education. He was of the opinion that education should be ideologically orientated and that any education which was neutral towards religion was evil and satanic. His advice to the Muslim nation was that if they sought inspiration from Islam, they could assemble their scattered forces, regain their lost integrity and thereby save themselves from complete annihilation.[8]

The Quran has very clearly laid down this objective of Islam in these words: 'It is He who has sent among the unlettered ones a Messenger from among themselves, to recite to them His Signs, to purify them and to teach them the Book and Wisdom, although they had been before in manifest error.'[9]

The Quran further clarifies this point while explaining the function of the Prophets. 'We indeed sent Our Messengers with clear proofs, and sent down with them the Book and the Balance (of Right and Wrong), that mankind may stand forth in justice.'[10]

Thus the mission of the Prophets was to educate the people, lead them to the ways of Allah—in righteousness and the establishment of a just and healthy society. The purpose of education is, therefore, to discharge this prophetic function—to educate the people in the religion of Islam, inspire them with its message and ideals, and prepare them for a fully developed life.

Islamic Ideal of Education

The acquisition of knowledge and the purification of self are the two essential ingredients of the Islamic system of education. The source of all knowledge is Allah who gives knowledge to mankind through His Messengers. The Messengers educate mankind in Islamic ideals, and purify it and prepare it for the establishment of justice, benevolence and goodness in society. This is the basic principle of Islamic education.

Islamic education gives importance to both knowledge and training and regards both indispensable to its objective. It considers knowledge and the purification of self (through training) as essential elements in its system of education. That is why knowledge and character-building are considered two sides of the same coin.

Islamic education inspires young men to accept with deep conviction the philosophy and ideology of Islam on an individual as well as a collective level. It prepares the young generation in Islamic ideology and Islamic philosophy so as to fulfil the mission of the Prophet—to propagate the Message of Islam and establish a pure, just and healthy social system.

Thus the main function of Islamic education is to educate the young generation in the Divine religion of Islam, to develop in them the spirit and ideals of this religion and to prepare them for a missionary life in the service of Islam. In the pursuit of this ideal, it is necessary to explain the Islamic viewpoint on the teaching of each and every subject. Before Western languages and sciences are taught to the young generation of Muslims particular care should be taken to ensure that un-Islamic (i.e. immoral, obscene, and irreligious) subjects are properly scrutinized and discarded. Islamic culture, history and ideals should be described and depicted at each stage in the teaching of foreign languages and the sciences so that Muslim students are not influenced by Western culture and Western ways of life. Similarly, those parts of textbooks and supplementary books which depict immoral or obscene stories or incidents and present irreligious, liberal views should be deleted.

Likewise in the teaching of science the students should be reminded of the concept of Tawhid, Allah, and that He is One and He is the Creator as well as the Controller of all the Universe and its physical laws. It should be put before them at each stage that He is the Final Cause of all causes.

The Main Characteristics of the Islamic Educational System

The Islamic Educational system has the following main characteristics:

1. *Acquisition of Knowledge.* Basic Islamic teaching is compulsory for every man and woman. Every Messenger of Allah was given knowledge of this before everything else. Muhammad (Peace be upon Him), the Prophet, received the very first revelation which commanded him to acquire knowledge. 'Read: In the name of your Lord and Sustainer, who created—created man out of a mere clot of congealed blood.'[11]

Thus in very simple words, the basic message of Islam is given to the Prophet Muhammad in his first revelation which proclaims it the duty of the Messenger and all his followers to acquire knowledge of their Lord (i.e. Islam) and spread it among other people. The Holy Prophet himself declared that the 'acquisition of knowledge is the duty of every man and woman.'[12]

2. *Imparting of Knowledge.* The first duty leads to the second, which is the teaching of knowledge. It is an important feature of the Islamic educational system that it makes it essential for Muslims to impart to other people knowledge which they have acquired. 'Acquire knowledge and teach other people.'[13]

3. *Moral Values.* Spiritual and moral values are emphasized and given extraordinary importance. No efforts are spared to uphold and maintain these values under all circumstances. This was emphasized by the Holy Prophet when he said, 'I am sent to perfect all moral values'.[14]

On another occasion the Holy Prophet said, 'People will come to you to acquire knowledge from all directions, teach them good morals.'[15]

4. *The Pleasure of Allah and the Public Good.* The knowledge is acquired and imparted to others not for monetary gain but for the good and welfare of society, and also merely for the pleasure of Allah. This view is based on many sayings of the Holy Prophet quoted by Abu Daud, Ibne Majah, Ahmed, Tirmizi and Darmi.

5. *The quest for knowledge becomes widespread.* All people, children and adults, literates and illiterates, are encouraged to seek knowledge. Educational facilities such as libraries, reading rooms and educational debates are provided so that people can continue their studies throughout life. It is reported that the Holy Prophet said,

'A believer's belly never gets full with knowledge, he keeps on storing it until he reaches the end of his life.'

6. *Education according to the Suitability of the Pupil.* In the early days of Islam, education was imparted according to the age, ability and aptitude of the child, and every effort was made to render the process of education easier for him. The Holy Prophet had established the basic principle by saying, 'Provide ease and do not put people to hardship; give good news and do not make them abhor you.'[16] Ali (MGBH), the fourth Caliph, elaborated the same principle in these words, 'Hearts of people have desires and aptitudes, sometimes they are ready to listen and at other times they are not. Enter into people's hearts through their aptitudes. Talk to them when they are ready to listen for the condition of the heart is such that if you force it to something, then it becomes blind (and refuses to accept it)'.[17]

7. *Development of Personality.* The natural talents and personal skills of each student are given ample opportunities to develop and to serve the community as each child is regarded a trust from Allah and all his physical and mental capacities and powers as a gift from Him. No stone is left unturned to provide facilities for the proper and full growth and development of the personality of each child. The whole Islamic system and its various organs are employed to direct each child to its right course —Islam.

8. *Emphasis on Action and Responsibilities.* Every student is inspired and persuaded to put into practice his knowledge; for mere knowledge is of very little use, as is pointed out by the Holy Prophet: 'Knowledge is of two types, one that goes straight from the tongue into the heart. This is beneficial and useful knowledge. The other which stays with the tongue and will testify against man in the Court of Allah.'[18]

The Islamic Educational system also imparts to each student a true knowledge of his responsibilities to the individual, to the family and to society and trains him to fulfil these in accordance with the Commandment of Allah and His Messenger.

Problems of Curriculum and Syllabus

The purpose of education determines the nature and contents of the curriculum and of each syllabus. If the purpose of education is secularism, then the basis of its whole syllabus will be irreligious and secular, and Allah and His Guidance will form no part of it. If the purpose of education is communism, then atheistic philosophy will colour the entire curriculum without any mention of Allah. The purpose of the education of a people determines the direction of its curriculum and syllabuses.

As Islamic education is ideologically orientated, the nature and contents of its curriculum and syllabuses will also be ideologically orientated. The beliefs and ideals of Islam will, therefore, determine its nature and contents.

1. *Tawhid (Unity of God)*. Allah is the Creator, Cherisher, Master and Sovereign of the earth and the whole Universe. All human beings are His servants and, therefore, subject to His Laws. They are not independent beings who came into existence without any Creator. They are obliged to obey Him.

2. *Risalat (Prophet-hood)*. Allah has sent His Messengers for the guidance of man. Muhammad (peace be upon him) is the last Messenger of Allah. Mankind can receive true and everlasting guidance only from His last Prophet and establish a system of Truth, Justice and Goodness on the earth.

3. *Akhirah (Life Harvester)*. All human beings are destined to die and one day stand trial before their Lord for their omissions and commissions. The obedient and righteous will be awarded with permanent life in the Paradise, while the rebels and wicked will be punished with a permanent life in the Hell.

4. *Concept of Khilafat (Vicegerent)*. The earth and the universe and all that is in it belong to Allah, and man is His Vicegerent on earth. Therefore, the right attitude and course for man is to live here as His obedient servant and obey His Commands. Encourage good, forbid evil and establish justice, benevolence and goodness on earth.

The curriculum and syllabuses should be designed on these lines. The basic doctrines of Islam should be taught in such a way that their meaning, purpose and bearing upon individual and social life is fully understood by students.

These should also be taught the Islamic values of morality, the nature and content of Islamic culture, and the duties and nature of their mission as Muslims.

Education should give special emphasis to the development of the individual personality of the student on proper, balanced lines. Islam stands for the golden mean and its ideal is the development of a balanced personality —growth of the individual personality along with a sense of social responsibility.

Another feature of the curriculum should be its emphasis upon the character-building of the student, for 'character training is closely linked with the conception of school as a society.'[19] Islam lays great stress on good deeds, and unless education builds up good character it will never achieve its real purpose. One of the fundamental functions of the Prophet is to purify human life and build good character.

As basic traits of character are formed in the early stages of life, school education can play an important role in building up the character of the child. It is, therefore, absolutely necessary that the school curriculum should be designed to mould the character of the child on the Islamic pattern. Imam Ghazzali has rightly pointed out that 'Education must not only seek to fill the young mind with knowledge, but must, at the same time, stimulate the child's moral character and stimulate him to the obligations of social life.'

The ideal character for a Muslim is that of the Holy Prophet Muhammad (PBUH). 'Indeed in the life of the Prophet of Allah you have the best example to follow.'[20] It is desirable that important incidents from the life of the Holy Prophet should be quoted at all stages of school education. These should be supplemented by examples from the lives of the Companions of the Holy Prophet.

Islam stands for life-fulfilment and induces its followers to seek the best of both worlds. Our education, therefore, prepares our young generation for the struggle of life. It gives young people an education to earn an honest and decent living, trains them in the arts and crafts of living and caters to the multifarious economic, social and scientific needs of the community.

NOTES

1. Lippman, Walter, 'The State of Education in this Troubled World', Speech, January 15, 1941, page 200.
2. Titmus, Harold H., Living Issues in Philosophy, New York, 1953, pages 420–431.
3. M. V. C. Jeffreys, Glanon, 'An Inquiry into the Aims of Education', Pitman, London, 1950, page 61.
4. Current History, September 1958, page 174.
5. Moberly, Sir Walter, 'The Crises in the University', London, 1949, page 70.

6. Vide, Hughes, 'Education: Some Fundamental Problems', page 86.

7. Sayyidain, K. G., 'Iqbal's Educational Philosophy', Lahore, 1942, page 99.

8. Iqbal, 'Statements and Speeches', Lahore, 1948, pages 35–36.

9. Quran, 62:2.

10. Quran, 57:25.

11. Quran, 96:1–2.

12. Hadith.

13. Hadith.

14. Hadith, Muatta, Imam Malik.

15. Hadith, Tirmizi.

16. Hadith.

17. Kitab-al-khyraj, Abu Yusuf.

18. Darmi.

19. Professor Smith, W. O. Lester, 'Education: An Introductory Survey', Pelican, 1958, page 25.

20. Quran, 33:21.

Chapter Six

Religious Education for Muslim Children in Great Britain: Guidelines and Syllabus

S. A. Ashraf

Syed Ali Ashraf was born in Bengal in 1925, and educated at Dacca (M.A. in English) and Cambridge University (B.A. Hons., M.A. and Ph.D.), was a secretary of the First World Conference on Muslim Education held at Mecca in 1977. At present he is Professor of English and Secretary of the Follow-Up Committee of that Conference at King Abdulaziz University, Jeddah. Previously he was Professor and Head of the Department of English, King Abdulaziz University, Mecca (1974–77); Visiting Fellow, Clare Hall, Cambridge (1973–74); Reader and Head, (1956–65) Professor and Head, Karachi University English Department (1965–72); Reader and Head, English Department, Rajshahi University (1954–56). He was also a Visiting Professor at Harvard University. Summer 1971, and at New Brunswick University, Canada, Summer 1974. His publications include: (in English): *T. S. Eliot Through Pakistani Eyes; New Harmony* (an anthology of Pakistani poetry in English); *Muslim Tradition in Bengali Literature, Homage to Nazrul Islam; Venture* (a quarterly, then a bi-annual journal of English language and literature, 1958–72); *Bengali Literary Review* (1971–73); (in Bengali); *Kavya Parichay* (a comparative study of Western and Eastern Poetics); *Kavya-Sankalan* (an edition of Golam Mostata's poems with an introduction); two books of Bengali poems *Chaitra Jakhan* and *Visangati*.

Note. This article was prepared by Dr. Ashraf for the Education Committee of the Union of Muslim Organisations which discussed, adopted, and published it as a U.M.O. pamphlet.

Guidelines

1. Religious Education: Meaning

Religious education means the teaching of religion as a comprehensive way of life. Pure 'theological training' or what may be called 'religious instruction' —that is, the training that makes a child aware of how to

100

say prayers, how to fast, how to pay *zakat* and how to perform *Hajj* — is differentiated by Muslims in Great Britain from 'religious education' by which is meant the moral and spiritual training of the child. This differentiation is not possible when we teach Islam since the teaching of Islam means the teaching of both aspects simultaneously. Together they cultivate an attitude to life without which 'religious education' becomes a mode of imparting information about religion rather than a means of cultivating a religious attitude to life. The term 'religious education', therefore, means religious instruction as well as moral and spiritual training of children. Children should be taught not only the tenets of Islam as rituals and formulae but also the moral and spiritual principles which provide the basic foundation of those tenets. In other words, though apparently religious education may be separated from religious instruction or from the teaching of *Fiqh* or the rules and regulations of Islamic tenets, they must be shown in practice to be integrally related to each other. That is why, both parents and teachers should know and practise Islam and not segregate knowledge from practice.

2. Graded Courses of Study

The practice of parents and teachers needs to be complemented and strengthened by the text books that they will use or the children are expected to read. Several books have already been produced in English to teach the formal, ritualistic, juridical or theological and historical aspects of Islam. But there are few well-written books for children of different age groups. Series are needed in English in which themes and styles are graded to suit the mental growth of children. This means that books dealing with the moral and spiritual aspects of Islam are so integrated with the courses of study dealing with the formal rules and regulations of Islam and the study of the Holy Quran and the Hadith that both together form an integrated and comprehensive course for different age groups.

These books should be graded to suit the following age groups:

Primary–Infant: 5 and 6;
Primary–Junior: 7 to 11;
Secondary: 11+ to 16;
6th Form: 16 to 18.

3. Primary–Infants

(a) Narratives of Concrete Historical Incidents

Children learn more by example than by precept. Parents and teachers
are or ought to be the best models for them. True current events and
stories of eminent people or news even of people round about them
affect their sensibility when these are presented to them in simple
narrative form. True stories of good and evil and the ultimate victory
of good over evil always appeal to young minds. The events which
show the Mercy of Allah the Almighty, the Generosity and Blessings
of Allah the Almighty and His Prophet, peace and blessings of Allah
the Almighty be on him, and the companions of the Prophet may,
therefore, be narrated with great enjoyment. As little children do not
have the patience to listen to long tales, long narratives should be
avoided.

(b) Pictorial and Descriptive Books and Nursery Rhymes

Other books suitable for this age group are of the pictorial and
descriptive type. Brief descriptive extracts may be read out of them.
These should accompany pictures given in the books depicting hills,
plains, rivers, oceans, trees and flowers. Nursery rhymes may also
accompany these pictures. Both the comments and the rhymes should
make children wonder at the glory, beauty and variety of earth and
the universe to make them feel the glory and greatness of Allah the
Almighty.

(c) Practical Training

As children are too small to understand any abstract concept, the only
form of religious teaching that can be imparted is by making them
imitate the parents and teachers and by conditioning their minds.
They should learn by heart the *Arabic* version of the *Kalima* and
through the question-answer method realize that they are Muslims,
their religion is Islam, their Prophet is Muhammad, peace and
blessings of Allah the Almighty be on him and that Allah the Almighty

and His Prophet, love us and we should love and respect them and obey them.

4. Junior

(a) *Basic Knowledge of Islam*

By the age of seven children should know how to perform *wadu* and have some basic knowledge about prayers, fasting and *Hajj*. By 11 years of age, they should know all the forms of prayer, learn all the *Kalimas*, the *imans* (*Iman-Mufassal and Muzzammil*), text of the prayer (*salat*) including *Dua Qunut* and other *Duas*, and learn by heart *Surah Fatiha* and the last ten chapters of the Holy Quran and at least five Quranic *duas*. They should also know what is *Halal* and *Haram* in food, what is permitted and prohibited in dress and social functions and conduct. These may be presented in question-and-answer form.

As they are living in a non-Muslim environment, it is necessary for them to know about the Unity of Allah the Almighty and His Qualities. They should also know that from the time of the Prophet Adam, blessings of Allah the Almighty be on him, till the time of the Prophet Muhammad, blessings of Allah the Almighty be on him, many Prophets, blessings of Allah the Almighty be on them, have come to lead man along the right path. They all preached the same fundamental truth, i.e. Islam, which our Prophet finalized and completed. There are many religions of the world because later followers added or changed the original World of God and thus gave a twisted form to the religion preached by the Prophet. All the ideas cannot be discussed in detail because children would not be able to understand intellectual concepts. But they ought to get a broad, general idea about the place of Islam in the family of religions. The other ideas which they should imbibe by the time they reach the eleventh year are: the idea of life after death, the idea of the Last Day of Judgement, the idea that Allah the Almighty controls our Fate, but He has given Man freedom to choose between right and wrong. Therefore, Allah the Almighty gives us rewards for our good deeds and penalizes us for our evil deeds. Such a comprehensive course ought to be prepared.

(b) *Historical and Moral Sense through Quranic Narratives*

Between the ages of 7 and 11 a child ought, not only, to learn and start practising the basic tenets of Islam, but also to acquire some historical sense. To achieve this end Quranic narratives dealing with the most significant events in the history of mankind should be told. The second aspect that should be kept in mind in selecting these narratives is the relationship of a section of book to the historical background of the tenets of Islam.

With regard to the first type of narrative, the following should be included in any textbook that may be prepared: the creation of the universe; the angels and the jinns; the creation of man; the fall of man; the quarrel between the two sons of Adam; Prophet Noah's flood; the stories of Syedena Ibrahim; Syedena Ismail; Syedena Yusuf and Syedena Musa (peace and blessings of Allah the Almighty be upon them). It is better not to have many stories and to relate the life and activities of only a few major Prophets.

The second type of narratives should include the following: how the Kaaba, the first house of worship, was built so that students may become aware of the historical importance of this house and how this house becomes the central house of God for mankind and why it is the *Qibla*; the story of the sacrifice of Syedena Ismail by Syedena Ibrahim so that children realize that the story of the sacrifice of Isaac (Syedena Ishaq) is untrue and a later fabrication by the Jews and the rites and rituals of *Hajj* are historically as much significant as they are for the spiritual enlightenment of man; the story of *Me'raj* of the Prophet of Islam, peace be on him, and the significance of the five daily prayers; the story of the *Hijra* of the Prophet of Islam, peace be upon him, to Medina so that children may know when and how Medina became the first capital of the first truly Islamic state and when and how the Muslim calendar was arranged.

The third type of narrative should be exclusively from the life of Syedena Muhammad, peace be upon him, and from the lives of the first four Caliphs, the *Khulafa-i-Rashidoon*. More emphasis should be laid on the moral and spiritual aspects of these stories than on their historical aspect.

5. Secondary

This is by far the most crucial period in the mental development of children. It is a period of idealism as well as questioning, doubts, rebellion and frustrations. In modern times when the atmosphere of the society in the West is charged with anti-religious sentiments and attitudes, it is becoming increasingly difficult for our children to accept dogma and orthodoxy unquestioningly and obey authority with reverence. Only by making children see religion as a historical and spiritual reality, by showing that the basis of our culture is in absolute values that religion alone enunciates and provides, and by presenting Islam as a natural and psychologically acceptable reality may we build up within children the force that will resist evil powers and strengthen the forces of the good. They should be made to realize that if they choose relativism in place of absolute values, they will become morally, spiritually and intellectually thoroughly confused. In order to achieve this end the following types of books may be prescribed or prepared.

(a) Historical

The history of the known Prophets, that is the Prophets mentioned in the Holy Quran, should now be presented in a chronological order. It should also be made clear to children that the Holy Quran tells us that besides these Prophets many other Prophets were sent by Allah the Almighty to different parts of the world. This will make children realize that fundamentally 'Islam' or submission to the Will of Allah the Almighty, was the only religion preached by different Prophets. They all preached the Unity of Allah the Almighty, the concept of Prophethood and the Last Day of Judgement. Certain rites, rituals, and tenets were different. But time and again man abandoned true teachings and fabricated man-made concepts and regulations. We should also tell children that as the Holy Quran does not mention the names of many Prophets, it is not proper for anyone to make any conjecture about any well-known persons of the past and proclaim them as Prophets. Writers of such a book should confine their attention to the Prophets mentioned in the Holy Quran. The stress should be on the major Prophets mentioned in the Holy Quran in some detail. They are: Syedena Adam; Syedena Noah: Syedena Ibrahim; Syedena Ismail; Syedena Yusuf; Syedena Musa; Syedena Isa; and Syedena

Muhammad, peace and blessings of Allah the Almighty be on them all.

The difference between this book and one for junior students lies in the treatment of the subject. Whereas the book for juniors will be more like a story book, this one will be more like a history based on the Islamic concept of history according to which, though civilization has led man from a primitive stage of technology to a very sophisticated stage, in so far as the values on which human culture basically depends, human nature has not fundamentally changed since the days of Syedena Adam. Absolute values are not subject to change. That is why human history, according to the Holy Quran, is the story of man's repeated fall, suffering, punishment, regeneration through the Prophets and again recession and fall till the arrival of Muhammad, peace and blessings of Allah the Almighty be on him, the last and the greatest of all Prophets.

(i) *Life and activities of the Prophet of Islam*, the *Khulafa-ar-Rashidoon* and the two grandsons of the Prophet. The life of the Prophet, peace and blessings of Allah the Almighty be on him, should be presented so as to meet all the challenges of the Western, non-Muslim scholars. This book should end with the tragedy of Karbala (Iraq) where Imam Hussain, may Allah the Almighty be pleased with him, gave his life fighting to uphold the principles of Islam.

(ii) *Islamic Movements and the Leaders in the Muslim World: Past and Present.* This third book should complete the historical perspective by making children aware of the contrast process of regeneration going on in the Muslim society, a process in which *Mujaddids* play the dominant role. In the past, especially as long as the Muslims retained their dominance in the civilized world, the main role was that of religious and hence moral and spiritual reformers checking degeneration and revitalizing the Islamic forces. At present, especially in the context of the challenge of the dominant Western technological and secularist society and concepts, the role is political and social as well as moral and spiritual. The life and activities of the following leaders of thought should be included: Imam Ghazali; Shaikh Abdul Qadir Jilani; Shaikh Mueenuddin Chishti; Mujaddid Alf-e-Sani; Shaikh Badruddin Ahmad Sirhindi; Shah Waliullah; Jamaluddin Afghani; Muhannad Abduh; Muhammad Sanusi; Al-Hasan Al-Bannah; Allama Dr. Muhammad Iqbal; Maulana Muhammad Abdul Aleem Siddiqui. Among the leaders of the past, the following great thinkers should precede this discussion and be treated adequately: Imam Jafar Sadiq; Imam Abu Hanifa; Imam Malik; Imam Shafei; Imam Ahmad Ibn-Hambal; Ibn Arabi; Ibn Taimiya; Muhammad bin Abdul Wahab; Shaikh Osman Dan Fodio; and Said Nursi.

(b) Theological

(i) Study of the Holy Quran and Hadith

There should be three methods of studying the Holy Quran and the Hadith.

Firstly, as a follow-up to what was taught in Junior school, children should learn by heart some more *suras* and *ayats* of the Holy Quran such as: the first five *ayats* of the *Sura Baqara*; *ayat-ul-Kursi* or 2:255–257; 2:284–286 and some *suras* from the last section. At least ten Hadith related to man's duties and obligations to man should be studied carefully. Secondly would be a study of the *Tafsir of Suras: Fateha, Ar-Rahman, Duha, Inshirah, Teen* and the four *Quls*, i.e., *Kafirun, Ikhlas, Falaq* and *Nas*. Surah Fateha and the four *Quls* may be studied between the ages of 11 and 13; the rest may be added later.

Finally a study should be made of *ayats* and Hadith with reference to particular topics. These topics should be as follows: (i) *Tawhid*; (ii) *Risalat*; (iii) *Revelation*; (iv) *Akhira*; (v) *Huquq-Allah*; (vi) *Huquq-al-Ibad*; (vii) *Ibadah-Salat, Saum, Hajj, Zakat, Jihad*.

This should be possible if a book is prepared with these basic concepts as the themes and the *ayats* and Hadith are used to illustrate the themes.

(ii) Islam and Other Religions and Ideologies

Students at this stage should be confronted with the task of realizing in what way Islam is superior to all other religions and ideologies, in what way it is the most liberal as well as the most comprehensive way of life, how it is the most orthodox and at the same time the most advanced form of ideal. They should be allowed to compare Islam with other forms of religion and all new ideologies, especially the humanistic ideology of Humanism and Marxism. Those who prepare such a text book should keep in mind the following basic principles:

(i) All religions originally came from God Who gave man the same basic ideals and beliefs: belief in One God and the Last Day; belief in a God-given code of life enjoining Man to do good and to keep away from bad deeds; and, lastly, belief in whatever was revealed to all the Prophets;

(ii) At the same time, although other religious codes were sent to certain races or peoples Islam was sent for entire humanity;

(iii) Islam does not deny all previous revelations but contends that they have been adulterated by those who believe in those revelations. Islam is the most inclusive of all religions. It also purifies all old codes, expands and through the Holy Quran completes the cycle of revelations;

(iv) Islam is the most humanistic code of life because its concept of man is the highest and noblest ever conceived; hence the goal for mankind set by Islam is the best conceivable goal for man to aspire to.

(c) Cultural

(I) Muslim Civilization: Past and Present

The last two years of Secondary education should be devoted to an appraisal and full appreciation of Muslim culture and of Muslim contribution to modern civilization. This contribution has to be assessed from two points of view: the point of view of the historian who looks at past contributions and finds out how modern Western civilization and its culture are indebted to the growth and spread of Islam; and the point of view of a modern Muslim thinker who wants to find how Muslim culture, based on the Islamic concept of values, can resist the onslaught of technological dehumanization and establish man's position as the vicegerent of Allah the Almighty on earth. Islam asserts that civilizations go on changing because of the evolution of the instruments of civilization but the total nature of human personality does not change. There can only be variations on the emphasis that is laid on certain aspects of human personality. Absolute values which are nothing but the Attributes of Allah the Almighty, do not change. Non-religious, and even anti-religious attitudes are at the root of the secularist mentality against which young minds must be prepared.

(II) *Institutionalization*

The culture of a society is always manifested through some socio-cultural institutions. These institutions provide the society with certain unifying symbols and a number of traditions that keep the society together through different periods of social changes. These socio-cultural institutions should be presented to boys and girls in their historical perspective. The best method would be to ask them to undertake projects in which archaeological, architectural, historical, philosophical or artistic, or technical knowledge may be used. Through painting, collection of pictures, or cards, through the preparation of charts or a variety of techniques these projects may be completed by students. The following are the major institutions of the Muslim society on which this work may be done:

(i) *Religious Institutions*

Mosque, Madrassah, Khanqah;
Imam, Ulama, Sufis;
Tafsirs, The Hadith Collections, Fiqh;
Philosophy, Tasawwuf;
Shariah and Tariqah.
While working on this project they should see the inter-relationships between people and between institutions.

(ii) *Social Institutions*

Family as the basic unit;
Rights and duties of man and woman;
Relation between man and woman, husband and wife, parents and children, orphans and a society, one member and another of a society.
The adjustment and balance between one relationship and another and the relationship between man and God through the consideration that all activities are undertaken by an individual or society in order to please God and not the individual himself.

109

The social aspects of religious rituals may thus be studied and presented through discussions, seminars, write-ups, posters and charts.

(iii) *Political and Economic Institutions*

The evolution of these institutions during the life-time of the Prophet, peace be upon him, and the first four Caliphs;
Principles derived from the Holy Quran and the Sunnah.

(iv) *Education*

A brief account of the evolution of the system from the inception of Islam till the fall of Baghdad may be given.
The basic principles: Allah the Almighty is the Source of all knowledge hence no human knowledge can ever be all-complete;
No barrier to the acquisition of knowledge. Any knowledge that leads man away from the path of goodness, righteousness and nearness to Allah the Almighty is knowledge misused and not seen in the correct perspective of the complete knowledge of Allah the Almighty.

(v) *Fine Arts; Architecture; Painting; Literature*

Various projects can be undertaken to make students familiar with and appreciate fine art from both the historical and the Islamic point of view.

6. 'A' Level 16 to 18

This is the last stage of adolescence and the beginning of mental maturity. It is time for children to go beyond historical facts and social evolution into the region of the conceptual analysis of the religion. They should also see the importance and relevance of Islam for the modern man. This study should be divided into four parts:
Part I:
Islam as a religion: Conceptual analysis;
Part II:
Social and moral foundations of Islam;

110

Part III:
Islam as a bulwark against modern atheistic concepts;
Part IV:
Final realization of man's own greatness through Islam.

Part I: Islam as a Religion

Conceptual Analysis: Islam claims that there has always been ONE religion — that which leads man to submit his will to the Divine Will. Through this concept has to some extent been explained at the secondary level when students are told to compare Islam with other religions and ideologies, at the 'A' level, discussion will lead students into the fundamentals of Islam including the concept of Tawhid, *Risalat* and Vicegerency of man on the earth.

Tawhid or the Unity of Allah the Almighty is integrally related to the unity of religious and hence to the similarity of revelations and the code for mankind. *Risalat* or Prophethood is tied up with their concept of unity and hence all the Prophets preached the same Islam. The finality of the Prophet of Islam indicates the mental maturity reached by man and also the journey of this creation towards Doomsday. Man as the vicegerent of God on this earth indicates the role that man has to play in this Universe, the greatness that he might achieve if he follows the rules and regulations given by Allah the Almighty and also the fear of punishment and suffering for wrong deeds. All these discussions should be related to the two psychological aspects of the human personality referred to in the Holy Quran, *Ruh* (Spirit) and *Nafs* (Self).

Part II: Islam as a Social and Moral Code of Life

The social and moral aspects of life are closely related to man's relation with Allah the Almighty and his own after-life. Secularism segregates the secular and the spiritual. Islam integrates the two and considers that which is regarded by the secularists as secular as fully dependent on the Divine ingrained in the human spirit. In the West morality is now generally considered relative to social evolution. But Islam looks at society from the absolute concept of man and his relation to Allah the Almighty; hence the evolution of

111

society does not mean the continuous birth of ever new societies but changes of, emphasis in different generations on different aspects of human personality. The Islamic moral code based on absolute values should then be defined.

Part III: Islam as a Bulwark against Modern Atheistic Concepts

Islam versus humanism; Religious attitudes versus scientific attitudes. Humanism and Scientific attitudes explain the emergence in the West of different kinds of philosophy and concepts including the concepts of capitalism, communism, socialism and scientific humanism. These are all partial and hence conflicting. Islam is the most comprehensive code for the modern man.

7. Conclusion

Children who have gone through the lessons prepared along the guidelines given above are expected to have built within themselves the positive power to resist the disintegrating and degenerating forces of modern civilization and gain certainty and peace of mind. He or she is expected to grow up as a balanced personality and not as a person having too much bias in one direction or the other. After going through all the situations that a modern man is expected to encounter in life, after being exposed to conflicting forces while being kept aware of the positive values of religion and after being able to compare the values of faith and goodness against the disillusionment of modern life, these children, God willing, should grow up with deep faith and with the desire to carry on a campaign for true *Jihad* (struggle in the path of Allah the Almighty). Religious Education will then be not just the acquisition of intellectual information about Islam, but an education conducive to the growth of a strongly religious personality.

Part 2   *Teacher Education*

Edited by Professor Nabi Ahmed Baloch

Preface

A group of sixteen member scholars (see Appendix A) participated in the deliberation of 'Committee —B6 on Teacher Education' of the First World Conference on Muslim Education in accordance with its scheduled programme. Some members presented Papers while others expressed their views during the course of discussions. Final recommendations were drawn up by the whole Committee.

The Introduction reflects the general trend of thought of the Committee based on the Papers presented and on the viewpoints expressed during discussions. More specific and detailed views are to be found in the individual Papers, which follow.

The edited text of the Papers is based on the original scripts, and those in Arabic are reproduced in almost literal English translations. In editing, care has been taken to see that the substance of each argument is presented as clearly as possible. The recommendations of the Committee are given in Appendix B in their original English text.

N. A. Baloch
Chairman of Committee on Teacher Education,
The First World Conference on Muslim Education

Introduction

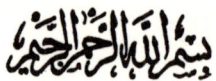

1. The 'education and preparation of teachers' is the central, most crucial and most challenging problem involved in the reconstruction of any educational system. The main objective of the First World Conference on Muslim Education held in Mecca in 1977 was to identify and formulate such principles and policies as would be instrumental in changing the present individual educational systems into systems which were truly 'Islamic' in character. Secondly, it was also recognized that, among other steps, teachers should spearhead this change and, therefore, all teachers trained and untrained, should be specially made aware of the 'concepts and methods' whereby Islamic beliefs and ideas can be instilled 'into the minds' of the pupils. Thus, while more detailed guidelines regarding the nature and the objectives of an 'Islamic System of Education' were expected to emerge from the deliberations of the different committees and of the conference as a whole, these two basic view-points had already been underlined in the preparatory material for the Conference.

2. Defining the objectives of teacher education or the role of the teacher in Muslim society, is not a question of evolving a separate theoretical formula. There can be no 'theory of teacher education' *apart from* the 'educational system' itself. So far as the Islamic Educational System is concerned, teacher education is the very heart and soul of it, and the role of the teacher is that of an active and committed member of Muslim society. In 'modern' educational systems, education represents the principles and policies formulated mainly by administrators, which are to be implemented by teachers and other educational workers. Thus the preparation of teachers and their work is considered within the framework of implementation. Such a notion does not wholly conform to the spirit of Islamic Education wherein the teacher becomes the leader and the guide in developing educational ideas and institutions, plans and procedures. 'Educational Effort' in Islam is in itself an 'Implementation Effort' for the establishment and development of a model Muslim Society. The preparation and the work of teachers are an integral part of the whole

116

educational effort. There is no dichotomy between the 'teacher' and the 'administrator', as is found in modern education systems.

3. The principles and purposes of Islamic Education, including those of Teacher Education, are not to be regarded as mere rational formulations and eloquent statements, but are to be made and accepted as 'operative principles' for a programme of action. Statements as such are static in their verbal forms, and only become dynamic and meaningful when they guide action. Policy statements without actual implementation represent a 'dualism' between *qual* and *fa'l* which is ruled out in the Islamic System. This calls for a *commitment* to make the purposes, principles and the policies operative throughout the entire educational effort (the system) in a Muslim society.

4. Since the education of teachers is an integral part of the educational system, its objectives remain the same as those of Islamic Education, which each Muslim country (constituting a specific Unit of the Islamic Community or *Ummah*) has to formulate and accept as a programme for practical action. In this formulation, the main 'Guiding Principles' for the System must be based upon the 'Fundamental Sources' of the Islamic Community, the Holy Quran and the Sunnah of the Holy Prophet (Salem), while application of these principles is to be determined by the requirements of the particular Muslim country, beginning with its present needs, problems and conditions, and relating them to its continuous future development.

5. The objectives of teacher education in Muslim Societies should have a basic unity in fundamentals but variations in application. In order to determine the role of the teacher and the nature and objectives of teacher education, each country will have to:

(i) arrive at its own consensus regarding the Guiding Principles for the Educational System (to be derived from the Foundational Sources);

(ii) assess its own needs and problems in present conditions, and requirements for future development; and

(iii) determine its own 'strategy' of application in terms of specific objectives, policies and procedures to be followed in the light of the 'Guiding Principles'.

It is to be expected that serious thought on these lines in each home country will produce teacher education programmes valid in terms of Islamic educational objectives.

6. Since the Foundational Sources for deriving the Guiding Principles are the same and also the *basic* needs of each Unit of the Islamic Community (the Ummah) are similar in nature, this will provide a common denominator of unity for each System. However, there will be variations in the way the Guiding Principles are formulated and applied in each 'country model' of Islamic Education. 'Models' developed in different Muslim countries can be studied from time to time at international Islamic Community forums, such as the First World Conference, and the better and the more effective policies and procedures can be identified to enable each country to improve its own model. This in turn will lead to a further unity arising from a continuous search for 'the ideal model'.

7. All Muslim countries belong to developing areas of the world, and Muslim societies in most of those areas have been seriously affected, some even to the point of disintegration, mainly by the impact of foreign domination and modern developments. The need for survival, identity, independence and progress is now keenly felt in all these societies and although education can be a most effective instrument in solving their problems, Muslim countries are comparatively backward and have a low literacy rate. Education itself therefore, becomes the most urgent problem to be solved. Experience has shown that any type of education, indigenous or alien, will not help to solve the problem. It needs the *right type* of education, which is designated as Islamic Education and the reconstruction of which was the subject of the First World Conference on Muslim Education. This viewpoint was underlined in all the Papers read on Teacher Education. Other pressing problems are: promoting economic development, improving community health and sanitation, and developing competence in co-operation i.e. taking agreed and intelligent decisions on the management of the affairs of community and country. Therefore, each 'country model' of Islamic Education should be geared to the solution of such pressing problems.

8. A dynamic strategy of application is required in view of the changing needs, problems and conditions in each Muslim country. In general, a strategy for action involves planning and execution so that under given conditions specific objectives are successfully achieved. This comes within the domain of *al-hikmat* which guarantees excellence in achievement.

Specific achievement goals guide the actual education process in

118

terms of quality, quantity and direction, but the main responsibility for developing strategy lies with the teacher.

9. As a general guideline, the preparation of teachers should be directly related to the educational objectives to be achieved in the light of the basic Guiding Principles and the specific achievement goals set for different levels of learning. The main purpose of teacher education is, obviously, to produce good teachers, but this is not enough by itself. It becomes necessary to formulate policies which, by minimizing the problems and extending the essential facilities, create an environment which enables the good teacher to contribute best towards the achievement of educational goals. In an Islamic Educational System, the community is directly responsible for creating such conditions. The concept of a good teacher and the purposes and policies for teacher education may vary in different Muslim countries in terms of their own Guiding Principles and the specific achievement objectives as they affect needs, problems and conditions.

10. The purposes and policies for teacher education should be defined by each Muslim Society, but these must have the aim of producing the good teacher whose excellence is measured in terms of faith, belief, personal qualities of conduct and character, professional competence and the actual achievement. It is, however, necessary that a Muslim country should have a clear concept of excellence in its own teachers. To be able to visualize the distinctive role of the teacher in a given Muslim society, a question may be raised in a wider context: How does excellence in the teacher in a Muslim Society differ from excellence in the teacher in any other society? Policy makers in each Muslim country will have to find a satisfactory answer for themselves considering its implications for the preparation and the actual work and performance of teachers in the system. In this context, the need for proper recruitment and selection of teachers for Islamic Education was specially emphasized by the First World Conference members in their Papers and discussions on Teacher Education.

N. A. Baloch

Chapter One

Islamic Curriculum and the Teacher

M. Al-Aroosi

Muhammad Al-Aroosi was born in Mecca, Saudi, in 1940. He is Assistant Professor, King Abdulaziz University, the Sharia Faculty. He received his Ph.D from the University of Edinburgh, and his U.K. publications include researches on Matrimonial Relations, Islamic Sharia and Jurisprudence.

Introductory

Praise is due unto Allah alone. We ask for His succour and guidance. We also ask of His infinite bounty that He might make Islam wax mighty and prevail—its banners flying; and that Muslims should follow the path of righteousness and earn His pleasure.

Blessings and peace from Allah be upon His final messenger and seal of prophethood, Muhammad, the son of Abdullah, his kindred and his companions and disciples. Blessings and peace be equally upon all Allah's Messengers and Prophets.

Ours is a time when humanity, the world over, is passing through a period of anxiety and bewilderment. Humanity has quite manifestly suffered a loss of purpose and seems everywhere to be groping for some sense of direction. This is because it has lost real contact with the Divine and the guidance of its Creator. It has in fact gone quite a distance away from His chosen path of righteousness for its ultimate deliverance.

Humanity became unhappy and bewildered when mankind resorted to the worship of its own reason, then sought to worship the human body, and then the abstract matter out of which things palpable were assumed to have been made. Then came the worship of things imaginary, with fanciful names. This was indeed to go very far astray. Of these chimerical objects of worship one was historical inevitability (a philosophical muddle). Social and economic inevitabilities were

120

also deified and bequeathed to us as equally meretricious goddesses of false worship.

Following these fanciful will-of-the-wisps has made most men lose their vision and power of discernment. Human behaviour became like that of a somnambulist, and these deceptions bred the fond hope that there would be salvation and even happiness. But the garden path led to suffocation amidst flames and smoke. Humanity is now almost on the brink of self-destruction. Only some timely mercy from Allah can save the sons of man by calling on their hearts once more to rediscover and follow the right guidance of divine wisdom which leads no one astray.

The way of Allah is clear and open. Truth is calling at daybreak and at eventide: 'Come hither, this is the right road; there is no other'. But, it cannot be found and followed except by fully understanding and accepting the precepts of Islam. Islamic Education should link both mind and thought with Islam. This should in turn inspire heart and psyche to find their true direction upon the straight road which is the correct highway for humanity's march to its real destination.

Curriculum and the teacher are the cornerstones of Islamic education. True, there are other contributory factors but these are its indispensable pillars. It is the primary duty of Muslims to be on the lookout for those teachers who corrupt those whom they teach. I only have to call attention to what Gibb, the orientalist, has said in the introduction to his book called *Whither Islam*:

'The work of contemporary education and journalism has influenced the Muslim World, even unconsciously, to such an extent that Muslims seem nowadays to behave as if they were of almost an entirely secular persuasion. This is really the heart of the matter as far as the marks of Western civilization on Islamic culture are concerned. In reality, Islam is fairly intact as a religious belief but as a dominating power over social life it has lost much of its value.

Take note also of what William Guildford has written in one of his reports:

'When the Quran and the city of Mecca disappear from the horizon of Arab countries, we can then see the Arab progressing on the path of our civilization from which only Muhammad and his Book have kept them away.'

Christian proselytism is now allied to two new dangers which threaten our contemporary life. These are communism and Zionism. They have joined hands to make war on Islam in many diabolical ways and with all the power that they can command. We are warning others of this new danger and are reminding everyone of the heavy responsibilities with which we are charged. For these we are all accountable before God and history.

It is for the sake of all this and because of our awareness of the paramount importance of the curriculum and the teacher in shaping the destinies of nations and peoples in moral performance and in knowledge, that we are broaching this subject. But it is a subject which cannot be adequately covered by a mere paper read out in a conference. It requires collective study undertaken in a spirit which is commensurate with the seriousness of the subject and its consequences. I have, however, presented in this paper those matters which, in my view are pointers for future research. The argument of this paper is under the following headings:

    I.   The Essentials of Islamic Education.
    II. A Brief Historical Background of Islamic Education.
    III. The Curriculum and the Teacher in the Present System.
    IV. Some suggestions for the Achievement of the Aims of Islamic education.

I. The Essentials of Islamic Education

Islamic education aims at creating a type of thinking and a pattern of study which should be the basis of human behaviour and its peculiar relation to all activities undertaken as prescribed by Islamic Jurisprudence. The whole purpose of the Islamic Sharia, the Way or Philosophy of Life, is to effect the greatest possible co-ordination between man and his God-given and native potentialities.

Islamic education is different from specialization in Islamic disciplines of the mind. The difference resides in the fact that Islamic education seeks to inculcate an honest motivation for human conduct. In other words, it seeks to shape motives according to the moral patterns laid down by Islamic philosophy and the ethical governance of life in its diverse manifestations and dimensions. This of course assumes the teaching of Islamic disciplines which define Islam as a belief and a way of life. Thus, the Muslim individual is given sufficient cultural nourishment for him to be able to call on Islam and defend it when necessary.

Specialization in the disciplines of Islam depends upon the effort

122

and the intellectual ability to acquire knowledge of Islamic beliefs and jurisprudence according to established methodology from its four original sources. These are: the Glorious Quran, the gracious Tradition of the Prophet, *ijmaa* or consensus of learned opinion, and *qias* which is a specialized kind of analogical deduction. The latter two sources include their products which are established according to the right precedent. However, this can never mean that the specialist should be negligent of any other aspect of Islamic education. On the contrary, the learner at that level is supposed to be a savant of Islam, or at least an *alim*, who is to be an example to be followed by other Muslims. First and foremost the specialist is a Muslim upon whom it is incumbent to be steadfast in his adherence to Islamic precepts and principles.

I do not mean to say that every student should attain a specialized knowledge of all these subjects. Students, however young, should be given a true and not a mis-shapen idea of Islam. In other words, knowledge of Islam should be genuine and authentic and should never be derived from untrue or unreliable sources. A student who has absorbed an unbalanced notion of Islam can become an easy victim of the present cultural onslaught on the lands of Islam. The endeavour to destroy Islam has never ceased since Islam began its spectacular advance and triumphed throughout most of the world.

Islamic education began in the lifetime of the final Prophet, who was the emissary of Allah to mankind. The Prophet was certainly the first educator in Islam, and an exemplary teacher for all times.

Islamic education was based from the very beginning on the Glorious Quran and the immaculate Sunnah. As the Quran is an authentic book which has never changed since the day of its revelation, it is not strange that Islam, which is based on it, should have its own unique pattern of education. Also it is not a bit surprising that this particular system of education should differ from all other systems.

From its beginning, Islamic education has been concerned with the education of the inner self and the purification of the Spirit on the one hand, and the cultivation of the Mind and the strengthening of the body on the other. It is an all-round form of education for the whole man, i.e. his intellect, spirit, religious life and his acquisition of knowledge. No part should be sacrificed in favour of another.

History records that the holy Prophet ransomed ten prisoners captured in the battle of Badr, on condition that every day one of them should teach ten Muslims to read and write. A well known recommendation of Caliph Umar Ibn al-Khattab, too, is that Muslims should teach their sons to swim and to handle bows and arrows effectively.

The Importance and Essentials of Religious Education

Religious education is of the utmost importance in bringing up the young and endowing them with the capacity for happiness in the future. It purifies souls and hearts, stimulates the conscience and encourages its recipients in virtuous habits and noble deportment. It is the sort of education which safeguards young hearts against the violent whims of desire and protects the young soul from the tyrannical sway of those passions and desires which can often lead to perdition. It lights the way for virtuous demeanour. Those who are blessed with this type of education become anxious to obey their Eternal Sovereign and Sustainer and to establish relations with their fellow men which are based on love, co-operation and sincere counsel. Moreover, it creates a strong sense of esprit de corps between fellow citizens which can stand the test of adversity, because its warp is the fraternity of kindred spirits and its weft is the covenant of hearts. It generated the basic culture which once made of the Arabs a daring and progressive nation; it became the torch of Islam to light the whole earth. It has its own methodology and procedure which provide opportunities for self renewal. In spite of its diversity, the methodology of religious education in Islam can be outlined as below:

(1) It is a planned system wherein subjects are defined and curricula specified.

(2) A good example is set by parents and the immediate environment of brothers, and sisters, relatives and teachers.

(3) A healthy religious atmosphere is ensured in the home, the school, the factory or the workshop.

(4) A charismatic society exists which is committed to religion as belief and as behaviour; and which naturally encourages virtuous behaviour but condemns vile and vicious ways.

Its Essentials

By essentials here we mean the basic principles which must be adhered to in choosing subjects for religious instruction, and in selecting the method of presenting them to pupils. Foremost among those principles are:

1. Islam has three dimensions — faith, knowledge, and behaviour. This calls for diversification of content so that the courses taught contain elements of each dimension at all stages of educational progress. This completeness is the guarantee that pupils will have a full Islamic education.

2. Many episodes from Islamic history can be aptly presented and can engender the right feelings by bringing out the significance of such events. This way of presenting history forges a constant link between the past and the present. Possible solutions to current problems can be obtained by referring to the inexhaustable fund of timeless wisdom which is to be found in Islamic experience.

   Religion is not just an accumulation of knowledge or acquisition of skill. It involves the spirit and the emotions. The success of a teacher cannot, therefore, be measured by his skill in imparting knowledge of biographies or of judgements and laws. It is rather to be measured by the extent to which he is able to set a good example upon his pupils' minds through correct and sincere beliefs. Religious knowledge can be of little value if it does not lead pupils to good deeds and worthy behaviour, or if it does not deter them from vice and shameful conduct.

3. Imitation and mimicry are manifestations of an old and deep-seated human instinct. Children like to imitate whatever action or attitude they see before them. Good and beautiful examples are just as capable of being imitated as bad and ugly ones. It is thus much more effective to instruct by example than by mere verbal enunciation of a precept. If the teacher does not present an exemplary conduct and character, religious instruction may well fail to refine his pupils' conduct. It does not follow automatically that he who is taught precepts praising the value of truthfulness will necessarily be a truthful person. However, good example rarely fails to impress, inspire and reinforce the precepts and principles communicated by the teacher in class.

Thus, if the school can become a place where pupils endeavour earnestly to live by the ideals of justice, honesty and truth, it can go a long way to becoming a model whereby pupils can live a good and happy life.

4. A teacher should not hesitate to call on all his knowledge and experience to elucidate a point in the lesson at hand. The particular lesson should be the pivotal point of interest, but not the only one. The importance of the teacher lies in awakening the pupil's whole personality to receive the precepts of Islam not as mere words to memorize but as a whole world of inspiring experience and exalted example. The teachers of Islamic knowledge should be equipped with a rich cultural background and also be blessed with a high, and inspiring moral character; for no one can really preach what his practice does not corroborate.

5. Every pupil, whatever his age, has religious feelings which are part of his make-up. The child is likely to be hurt, and even roused to anger, if someone questions his religious feelings. This should be a useful pedagogical deterrent to the use of brow-beating and physical force with the child.

6. Some pupils, both boys and girls, are often subjected to certain psychological stresses, crises and personal problems in life. They are prone to all sorts of mental and emotional imbalance, if they are not taken care of in the right manner and at the right time. A teacher in an Islamic system of education can do a great deal in this respect by encouraging his pupils to confide in him. A teacher can act like a wise and compassionate father who ministers to the psychic ailments of his young and perplexed children.

7. Due attention must be given to Islamic worship so that the young grow up in an atmosphere of judicious reverence and considerate behaviour towards their fellows.

II. A Brief Historical Background of Islamic Education

The beginning is traceable to the lifetime of the last Messenger (May Allah's blessings and peace be upon him). He was the first educator

126

at a time when no specified places for education existed. It is most probable that special gatherings were casually organized. At the Battle of Badr, many literate prisoners were taken from amongst the Quraish, and these were ransomed by giving lessons in literacy to the Muslims, especially the younger ones. These lessons were given outside the mosque, though not in any specified place.

Development of the Primary School (Kuttab)

After the time of the Prophet there emerged a system of primary schools which later evolved and became known as Katateeb (plural of *Kuttab*). In addition classes for private tuition were held by agreement between parents. A proof of this is Umar Ibn Khattab's injunction to Muslim parents that they should teach their sons specific knowledge and skills. It appears that *Hajjaj* represented an intermediate stage between private schooling for the privileged few, and public education for all children without exception. *Hajjaj* is specifically referred to as a children's teacher (*mu'allim al-sibyan*), i.e. a primary teacher by profession. According to Qazwini: 'Hajjaj began his career as a teacher of the young (*Lushaque*, which is a Persian word meaning "boys" or "pages").' This means that Hajjaj, in his former and more humble calling, had taken an important step in becoming a teacher, not only for the scions of the great, but also for all children of the community. Obviously, he was not a private tutor but a community teacher.

It was recommended that children should not be taught inside the mosque, because little boys could not be expected to care for their personal cleanliness. The Prophet (peace be upon him) had directed that mosques were to be kept absolutely clean, and the insane and the small children were to be kept out of them because they would blacken the walls and fail to control their bodily functions. The judgement of Iman Malik Ibn Anas is also a case in point. He wrote that children were not to be taught inside the mosque because mosques were to be kept immaculately clean according to the explicit injunctions of the Holy Prophet. He said that children should be kept out of mosques as much as possible and should be taught at special places adjacent to them. Accordingly, it became customary to build classrooms adjacent to, or in the neighbourhood of, mosques. This practice was in accordance with the best spirit of the Prophet's express injunction, whereby children could be kept near the mosque so that they could

127

enter it whenever they were fit and sufficiently clean for entry. In actual practice, teachers holding their classes in mosques allowed into their circles of lessons children who were old enough to be trusted with keeping themselves clean and free from filth.

Besides the *Kuttabs* which were adjacent to mosques, there were others which were situated in independent localities. Imam Shafi'y referred to such a school when he wrote that he grew up as a little orphan under his mother's care, and that she sent him first to the *Kuttab* and then to the Mosque school. 'When I completed the Quran to its last chapter, I was taken to the Mosque.'

Abul Qassim Al-Bulkhi had a *Kuttab* of 3000 pupils. In his reference to this school, Yaqut not only mentions its independent status apart from the mosque, but also speaks of its capacity to hold all that number in its spacious courtyard and rooms. For this reason, Bulkhi had to ride a donkey to be able to look after all this multitude of learners and supervise their progress. There was also another Bulkhi, Ah'mad Ibn Sahl (311 A.H.), a man of great learning, whose works exemplified the methodology of philosophers but whose style was more that of a literary man. He was a teacher of boys, but his learning led to further success.

The number of elementary schools (*Kuttabs*) and teachers increased considerably from the second century of the Hijra onwards. This rapid growth was a response to the great expansion of Islamic civilization, the main strength of which was education. The growth in the number of schools was so large that every village had its own school, and some had even more than one. Ibn Hayqal counted as many as 300 elementary school instructors (*Mu'allim' al-Sibyan*) in one locality.

Development of Primary Curriculum and Methodology

The principle of having a broad-based curriculum for an all-round growth of the learner was recognized in the educational policy laid down by Caliph Umar. In a circular which he sent to the urban communities in the Muslim dominions, he gave them the following directive: 'You are required to instruct your young in swimming and the equestrian art. You should also make them learn well-known proverbs, wise sayings and good poetry.' Ibn al-Kiram used to say: 'The best education that fathers can give their sons for their security is that they should teach them the Book, arithmetic and swimming.'

128

We have already referred to the curriculum for teaching the young as just a general programme. In the different regions of the Muslim world, different disciplines were emphasized. Ibn Khaldun has elucidated this in the chapter of his *Muqaddima* entitled 'The education of the young and the different policies adopted by the different urban centres of the Muslim world in dealing with it.'

Teaching the Holy Quran to the young is one of the religious commitments. The Muslim community in all the great cities had adopted this practice. Learning the Holy Quran, therefore, became the basis for further intellectual development.

The method of teaching the Quran differed in different regions. The people of the Maghrib (the western part of the contemporary Muslim world) opted for concentration on learning the Quran by heart, whilst paying special attention to the manner of reciting and writing it. No other subject was taught along with the Quran, not even Hadith or Fiqh. When *Kuttabs* were established and the *Hafizes* (those who had committed the Holy Quran to memory) began to work as instructors in them, the Quran became the pivotal point of all study. Other disciplines then followed in the wake of the Holy Book.

Ghazzali recommends that at the Maktab (elementary school), the child should first learn the Quran, then history, accounts and chronicles of saintly folk and their ways. Then he should be taught some rules of religion. To this, Ibn Misqaveh adds elements of arithmetic and some principles of Arabic Grammar. Jahez counsels that young children should not be overburdened with the rules of grammar. 'It suffices,' says he, 'that a youth should be taught to avoid the worst pitfalls and blunders; and to eschew the ways of men of the populace when they read letters aloud, declaim poetry or attempt some elegant description in what purports to be correct Arabic. Anything more than this essential knowledge is mere superfluity and the time spent could have been more profitably employed in learning things of greater import such as truthful narrative in chronology, proverbs, pithy sayings and well turned expressions.' Jahez also advises that the young pupil should be taught some arithmetic without bothering with either geometry or surveying. According to him, young learners should learn fair composition in familiar words and elegant turns of phrase; and should pursue the works and letters of accomplished writers in order to grasp their sense rather than mere word-meaning.

The people of Alandalus (Moorish Spain) had an educational policy of teaching the Quran and writing. They did not limit themselves to the Holy Quran alone, but used to teach elements of poetry and prose as well. They paid special attention to the laws of Arabic syntax and grammar, and to the improvement of calligraphy. This latter practice was their greatest concern.

The people of 'Ifriqia' ('Tunisians') taught the Quran with an admixture of the Hadith in most cases. They also busied themselves with the discussion of the principles (*Qawanin*) of the 'Sciences'. This meant the study of religious disciplines, and knowing by heart some questions concerning them. But their greatest concentration was on learning the Quran and the science of *Qira't* which studies how the different authorities on the Quran understood its words considering the range of differences between the diverse Arab dialects, differing grammatical predilections and the basic interpretations of the text. Their attention to handwriting derives from this particular disposition. The people of the Eastern Muslim world, 'the Mashriq', were also disposed towards mixed study. Instructors took special care to have girls know by heart 'Surat al-Nur' (The Sura of Light).

The curricula followed by private tutors within the palaces of Caliphs for the princes, or for the sons of the Ministers, chiefs and other well to do families varied considerably in accordance with the specific assignments of the privileged scholars. In the final analysis, these curricula sprang from the same fount from which public schools benefited. The purpose throughout was to provide the learner with a general culture according to a general pattern of understanding and knowledge, the basis of which was to keep close to, and be informed by, the precepts of Islam, and develop in the young minds the Islamic ethos. But education in palace establishments had some special features. The curriculum was chosen in consultation with the father of the child, who normally selected the subjects for the enlightenment of his heirs. Teachers within this realm were called Mu'addibs and not 'Muallim al-Sybian. They were tutors of a special calibre and their charges continued to study even beyond the age of adolescence. The students moved within their sequestered world from the level of Maktabs to the higher level of mosque schools (*Al-Madaris*).

The following extracts represent some examples of the types of curricula which had been worked out by some fathers for the guidance of their sons and tutors.

a. 'Umar Ibn'Utba said to his children's tutor: 'Let the improvement that you are to

130

impart to my children first be yours. That is because what you do will be in their eyes the good; and what you do not, the bad. Teach them the book of Allah and be careful not to overburden with what you teach them of it, lest they become inclined to abandon it. Do not, however, stop for any length of time teaching them the Quran lest they become altogether oblivious of it. Make them learn the most noble prose and the chastest of poetry. Do not carry them from one discipline to another before they have become fully conversant with the first; for, the crowding of words within one's comprehension is a cause of distraction and worry. Teach them the ways of the wise, and deter them from conversing with women. Do not at all lay stress on any shortcoming of mine, for I have entrusted them to your perfections and not to my deficiencies.' (aliqd al-Farid of Ibn Abdirabbin)
Isfahani; Muhadharat alUdaba

b. Hisham Abdul Malik said to al-Halaby when he employed him as tutor to his son: 'This son of mine is so precious to me as the part of my face which is betwixt mine eyes. I have entrusted him to thy care; look to the fear of Allah and acquit thee of thine charge. The first duty that I charge thee with is to teach him to know the Book of Allah. After that, teach him the best of poetry. Then take him on a studious tour across the tribal circuits of Arabia in order to select the choicest of their poetry for him to memorize. Then teach him the limits of what is permissible and that which is prohibited. Also let him learn orations and the chronicles of *Maghazi* (the battles for Islam).'

c. One of the worthiest models of such curricula was proposed and recommended by Harun al-Rashid to al-Ahmar the tutor of his son and heir, Amin. This runs as follows: 'Oh Ahmar! The Commander of the Faithful has entrusted thee with the fruit of His heart and the very essence of His soul. Let Thy hand be powerful over him; for, to obey Thee is his bounden duty. Be then up to the position, which the Commander of the Faithful hath made thine. Teach him to read the Quran, Chronicles of Islam and beyond, and let him be conversant with poetry. Take care to have him learn the Sunnah, the ways of speech and how to begin a discourse. Deter him from laughter, except in time of mirth. Inculcate him with respect for Bani Hashem, when they come to see him. Teach him to honour commanders of armies and other leaders when they seek his company. Let no moment pass without profit to him, but without saddening his heart and thus deadening his mind. Do not be too gentle to him, because that encourages idleness in him and makes him inured to it. Correct him as much as you can with gentleness. But if he responds not to that, take him with severity and harshness.'

The Madrasah (Higher Educational Institution)

The Maktabs (Primary Schools) continued to discharge their functions with credit until the rise of the higher schools, the Madrasahs, such as the following:

(1) Imam Abu Hatin al-Busti (315 A.H.) built a school at Bust. He provided this with a library and rooms for the students. He also arranged to supply students coming from far away with stipends and

food. Busti had collected all his works in that school for the use of his students, and most of these were read under his guidance.

(2) Shafii's built a private school at Nishapur. They were admirers of Imam Nishapuri, the great Hafiz (349 A.H.).

(3) To honour Imam al-Hatimi (362 A.H.), the dignitaries of Tehran built a school for teaching the Fiqh of Imam Shafii.

(4) The traditionalist, Imam Sheikh Abu Ali al-Huseini (393 A.H.), built a school for Hadith. This had as many as one thousand students from different parts of the world.

(5) Imam Ismail (396 A.H.) established two schools for teaching the *madhab* of Imam Shafi'i. He appointed Imam al-Isfraini to head the one and Imam al-Baqi to head the other.[1]

III. The Curriculum and the Teacher in the Present System

The above references show that different types of schools and educational institutions flourished in the third and fourth centuries of the Hijra. Such institutions developed in all parts of the Muslim world, and offered educational programmes to suit the environment of diverse regions. This was so until the time when schools were organized at different levels — primary, secondary and the higher level. In some parts of the Muslim world some *Kuttabs* continued as before, though they remained neglected. Colonialism had wrought havoc in the Muslim world by the introduction of missionary schools. This new factor was mainly responsible for the withering away of the *Kuttab* as an educational institution.

When education was divided during colonial domination, authentic Islamic education began to disappear from the Muslim world. The change to secular and scientific schools had been abrupt, without any attempt to ascertain the effectiveness of the indigenous scholols. Military and political invasion paved the way for the far more lethal invasion of minds, which had alarming effects on a number of Muslim countries.

It was then that Allah in His boundless mercy inspired some Muslim educationists to reintroduce Islamic education, but as yet it has not reached the desired standard. Only Saudi Arabia which remained free from colonial domination, has become a pioneer in the field of Islamic education.

This desired standard in education depends essentially on the quality of two factors, the teacher and the curriculum, although the role of the home and the media is also important. To achieve high educational standards, there must be proper coordination and mutual aid between the home, the school and the media.

The Curriculum

Each level of education has its own psychological and pedagogical problems. A primary school boy cannot face the same problems as the university student. This fact of education must influence our planning at all levels so that the system of Islamic education is properly organized. There should be no discrepancy between curricula and the psychological and intellectual level of the learner. Unless such discrepancies are eliminated, the result of our endeavours will be negative.

The ingredients of an Islamic curriculum are: *Tawhid, Fiqh* (Jurisprudence and religious principles), the Glorious Quran, the Hadith and Islamic History with a moral message in it. *Tawhid* reinforces faith and harmonizes the essentials of this discipline with nature. *Fiqh* teaches the judgements of the Islamic science of jurisprudence. The Holy Quran is the source and the justification of all knowledge, while the sciences of Tafsir and Hadith are the corner-stones of the fabric of this knowledge. The importance of educative chronicles for young minds is too obvious to need any special emphasis. It is not possible to go into detail in the limited space at our disposal. It is enough to give some indication of the aims and objectives of the Islamic curriculum.

In the light of what has been said, we may critically examine some segments for this purpose, for example, the Third Year Intermediate of the Girls School syllabus of the existing curriculum. They study the transitional forms and patterns of *Sharikat* (partnerships) and a general synopsis of contemporary partnerships and companies to show the relation of these latter to the four specified types of *sharika*.

In Saudi Arabia there are companies of diverse kinds employed in all the vital sectors of economic life in towns and villages. Factories of various kinds and establishments are based on such companies. There are soap, plastic, cement and shoe factories. There are others for building projects, for development, and for making roads. Others are for lighting and agriculture. All are based on the patterns established by Fiqh. But insurance companies are vain enterprises based on a fallacy. They involve risk and the appropriation of other people's money. This naturally leads to untoward and unwholesome results. The company operates as follows. A person makes contact with an insurance agent, and undertakes to pay the company by specified instalments. If he should pay all instalments and remain alive, he is entitled to all the sums he paid plus the profit specified by premiums. In case of death, the heirs are entitled to the same. This is what the text-book says. But there is no attempt to trace this kind of transaction to the principles of Fiqh, or to any one of the four acknowledged types of partnership. This makes the student learn merely by rote, thus widening the distance between his/her understanding and the realities of life. With all due respect to the teachers concerned, we think that many of these worthies do not know at all the basis on which modern companies are formed. Moreover, insurance companies are companies only in name; and they are of different kinds and their objectives and operations cannot really be understood except by the experts who have gone deep into the technicalities of their economic organization.

We do not mean to say that we approve of insurance companies. We propose to emphasize that the student should study things in the light of facts. He/she has a right to know why insurance companies are based on false principles. It does not suffice to say that insurance companies involve some kinds of risk and are therefore wrong. One must show how this risk is involved and in what way it is related to games of chance. The student should not be fed on scanty information or even less reasoning. His mind and heart must be persuaded that what is presented to him is true and reliable knowledge. It would have been far better if one of the four legitimate types of partnership or business association were fully explained in relation to a properly investigated contemporary form of it. In that case, the student would be satisfied with what he or she is taught, and would not tend to consider it jejune or immature.

In the syllabus of *Tawhid* for the same class, the prescribed text-book tries to focus attention on a subject under the heading, 'Discussion of what comes under the rubric of the elucidation of the meaning of the Quranic verse, which says: 'And they esteemed not Allah at His true worth. The whole earth and the heavens are but a handful to

134

Him on Doomsday folded up in His Right Hand. Glory be unto Him and far exalted above that which they associate with Him'.

Immediately after this the author cites a number of texts from the Hadith (Traditions of the Prophet).

The holy texts of the fully authenticated Hadith are all, no doubt, very true, and the way of our pious predecessors is known to be the best and most judicious. But these youngsters who are taught this cannot be expected to digest it all and understand it properly. This is food for the mature specialist, not for the learner and the fledgeling. Moreover much of what is cited in such texts may well seem to be at variance with the natural sciences that they have to study. The young mind and the raw soul cannot be supposed to be able to reconcile the apparent contradiction between the content of such holy texts and their elementary notions of science. Many teachers may lack the ability to reconcile the difference and keep the youngsters' mind at peace. This sort of situation is obviously fraught with danger for proper religious education.

It is more apt, even imperative, to concentrate so far as the subject of *Tawhid* is concerned, on rational demonstrations of the Oneness and Uniqueness of Allah. There are many corroborative and persuasive arguments in favour of Islamic beliefs which are within the scope and level of understanding of these younger boys and girls. These youngsters can have their minds enriched and enlarged with proper and reasonably plain expositions of Islamic belief. This mode of instruction can immunize their tender minds against the rough winds of cultural invasion and spiritual dislocation which materialists and their allies are only too keen to promote.

The truths and values of Islam can, and must be presented in an acceptable and benevolent manner so that the young should profit by what they are taught and absorb it. The enemies' arguments must also be presented so that their falsehoods can be reasonably and convincingly exposed and their apparent persuasiveness exploded.

The Teacher

Islamic education is not a matter of dictation. It is not just a matter of behaviour either. But it is a 'whole', comprising two integrating aspects. The first of these is that a suitable portion of Islamic beliefs and matters of law and morals should be taught in a manner which

135

enables the student to understand, to a reasonable degree, the essentials of Islam. The second aspect consists in training the student's mind in a scientific and rational manner so that he should be able to harmonize his behaviour with the morals, law and faith of Islam.

In view of this, it is obviously necessary to consider the role of the teacher for this essential discipline of Islamic education. It is not enough that such a teacher should be well-read in Islamic material, or that he should possess an insight into Islamic beliefs and fundamental judgements. In addition, he must be endowed with two essential qualities. Firstly, he should have true academic and intellectual capacity; that is, he should have a good grounding in the sciences of Islam and should be well read in the general culture of Islam. Secondly, he should have the moral ability to be able to educate his pupils in such a way that they will become fully aware of the perfect accord between their teacher's words and his actual behaviour. Teachers of other subjects, too, must be men and women with moral beliefs; for their function is to impart what they teach in a religiously healthy way which promotes growth of knowledge and development of the mind. The teacher's moral attitude has undoubtedly a far-reaching effect upon the minds of his young pupils. The relationship which is established between teacher and pupil throughout the year, and thereafter, must have a lasting impression.

Every member of the teaching staff of an Islamic educational institution has a great responsibility to his students, and this responsibility must be considered at the initial stage of teacher selection. This selection must be infallible so that anyone who is not committed to Islamic values and attitudes is not selected for the teaching profession, for the same reason that the employment of such teachers would run counter to the aims of Islamic education. Moreover, at the level of scientific instruction, such teachers could contribute enormously towards the creation of negative attitudes which would make nonsense of all our educational endeavour. It would be as if we were building paper palaces on sand or marking lines upon the surface of the sea. Destroying with one hand what the other hand is building can have nothing but dire consequences.

IV. Some Suggestions

In the light of what has been discussed, the following suggestions are put forward:

1. We must insist on intellectual harmonization between curricula and the different phases of education which meets our needs. At the same time we must equip the moral personality of the learner. The young must acquire scientific understanding upon which the future can be built.

2. We must meet the needs of both the specialist and the non-specialist. The non-specialist should be given only that which is commensurate with his mental capacity. Controversial and intricate questions should be reserved for the specialists. Presenting controversial matters to the young only confuses their minds.

3. There must be considerable concentration upon topical issues which are raised by the mass media. One must pay attention to atheistic and evangelistic currents of thought which are working adversely against Islam. This concentration must be logically ordered and scientifically planned so that all falsification and mendacity is thoroughly exposed.

4. Islamic education must be an obligatory and an essential basis of curricula in the Muslim world. But there should be careful and intelligent planning for this. The subjects presented must be in harmony with the level of understanding at the primary, secondary, college and University stages. In this respect, Universities or the Muslim world can profit by the good example set by Saudi Arabia. All must endeavour to build up the character of the Muslim community in a way that accords with the ethos of Islam. We want our universities to produce graduates who are deeply imbued with Faith but equally endowed with wisdom and perspicuity. They must be committed Muslims but urbane enough to be able to defend their religion in a rational and persuasive manner.

5. The teacher should be trained in the most judicious and effective way conceivable. He must be efficient and capable of presenting his information by the right method. His mind must be alert to all knowledge and any controversy currently in vogue. He must be endowed with the necessary wisdom to inspire confidence and trust and to provide intellectual and moral satisfaction. Last but not least, the teacher must be of exemplary character so that he can be the living embodiment of the Islamic education which he undertakes to

teach. The media should be fully informed about this educational policy and these must endeavour to corroborate it in every way. Television, radio and the cinema have a more attentive and impressionable audience amongst young men and women than they have among adults or older people, and directors should be the first to think seriously about any matter they present. What they transmit must be completely in agreement with the basis of Islamic education and the true foundations of the ethos of Islam. For, only thus can we hope for an educational policy based on and intelligent and progressive idea of adherence to Islam. It has to be realized that the media can be agents of moral degradation, or can provide strong moral support for Islam against evil.

May Allah be our Protector, our guide to success and our support. We pray to Him to bestow upon the workers for Islam the best reward within the infinite realm of His bounty.

All Glory be to Him, the Giver of felicity in endeavour and the Guide unto the straight Path.

NOTES

1. For reference, see (i) al-Baihaqi: *al-Mahasin wa al-Masawi*, and (ii) Asad Tals: *Educational Pedagogy in Islam*.

Chapter Two

Producing Teachers for Islamic Education

A. H. Khaldun Kinnany

Abdul Haleem Khaldun Kinnany was born in 1914 in Damascus, Syria. His degrees include M.A. Dip-in-Ed. (Paris) and Ph.D. (London). He has held various positions as teacher, educational administrator and University Professor in Syria up to 1952, from 1952 to 1975 he was Director of Higher Education of UNESCO and was responsible for UNESCO activities in Secondary Education and Teacher Training in the Arab World. He is at present in Paris in charge of the French branch of Rabita (World Muslim League of Saudi Arabia).

A. Islamic Education

Islamic Education has existed since the establishment of Islam, though its influence has fluctuated through periods of prosperity and periods of decline. If we examine it carefully we find that: (a) Its principles and aims offer the most suitable educational system for Muslims in this age. (b) It is an original and integral system by itself and need not be compared with current systems of education to prove its status or universality.

Among its many characteristics, the following are the most important:

(i) Islamic education is an education of faith and optimism. It is based on the fact that the Quran, the teachings of the Prophet (Peace be upon him), and the behaviour of the Prophet's companions, disciples and the Muslim 'ulama give the Muslim thinker and the Islamic community guidance on good and perfect conduct, the virtuous life, and salvation in the Hereafter.

(ii) Islamic education has a message. One of its aims is to unite Muslims in one coherent community, the *Ummah*, and prepare

139

them to disseminate the message of Islam. Therefore, it develops in the Muslim a sense of responsibility to himself, to his community, and to his God. This responsibility can grow only on a basis of freedom and dignity.

(iii) Islamic education is thorough and comprehensive; it is planned to bring about harmony, balance and integrity in a man's life as an individual in the Islamic community (*Ummah*).

(iv) It is meant to bring about harmony and solidarity:

    (a) in man's 'whole' being, by co-ordinating the needs of the body (its bursting vitality and violent instincts), the self (its conflicting aspects, its aspiration for perfection and righteousness, and its proneness to evil), the mind (its need for comprehension, thought and logic), and the will (which helps man to ensure his self-realization to carry out decisions, unless it falls victim to weakness and hesitation).

    (b) in his social environment, by co-ordinating his own interests and the interests of his community so that he will be able to serve his society and the *Ummah* faithfully and efficiently. It secures for the Muslim harmony and consistency between his spiritual life and the modern urban, material, technological life which he is obliged to live, so that he is able to contribute to society's development in the direction of the supreme ends defined by Islam.

    (c) in his relationship with life, nature, and the universe; on the one hand he is influenced by their laws, and on the other he can influence them if he knows how to gain control over them with the help and favour of God.

(v) Islamic education is an education for society and civilization. Undoubtedly, a Muslim may live the life of a recluse if he so chooses; but Islamic education needs a human community to crystalize its system and show how this is organized. To flourish, its needs the Muslim Community (*Ummah*). Besides being in favour of peace, tolerance, forgiveness and kindness, Islam emphasizes the need for a Muslim society to be strong and free, to have power and authority so that it governs people according to Islamic law.

In spite of all its merits, achievements, and fitness for our age, Islamic

140

education is still unknown to the majority of Muslims (and man is against what he does not know).

Bringing about harmony in a Muslim's personality and in his relationship with society and the universe, is not an easy task that can be achieved within a short period. It is the hardest task that a Muslim may face in this life, as it demands constant jihad (struggle) within himself, jihad with society to contribute to its amelioration and development, and jihad to achieve every noble effort which works for the good of mankind and for co-operation and brotherhood among nations. It is a difficult and noble task which has to be continued throughout a Muslim's life and as long as the Muslim Community (Ummah) exists.

It is therefore necessary for teachers to be fully acquainted with the nature and objectives of Islamic Education; to reveal its excellent aspects and transmit them to young people and to student teachers under training; to employ modern techniques of communication in the dissemination of Islamic education both in Muslim and in non-Muslim countries.

To be able to do this, it is necessary to train teachers according to the principles of Islam and in a way that reminds them of the achievements of their early predecessors in the service of Islam, and to qualify them to perform their teaching role in the best possible way.

B. Teachers in the Early Islamic Society

In the early stages of Islamic history, teachers contributed splendidly to the spread of the message of Islam. They had a high degree of understanding of their responsibility, and a wonderful ability to fulfil it through the course of centuries and under most varied conditions.

Before Islam, the role of Arabs in the making of world history was insignificant. Even the course of their own history was largely dominated and oriented by outsiders. With the advent of Islam, the Muslim *Ummah* came into being and established a brotherhood of nations in large areas of the world. Muslims entered upon the stage of human history and civilization, left their permanent imprint on 'the making of world history' and also directed world history in the service of the ideals of Islam.

It was through this active participation in making world history that the Muslim became aware that his heart was open to God. He called upon him to carry a noble and blissful message to mankind. He became anxious to prove himself worthy of that noble and beneficent mission and to spread it everywhere during his whole life time. He spent all his energies in giving guidance, faith and usefulness by making sacrifices to fulfil God's purpose. Teachers during that early period were none other than the brave soldiers who promulgated the message of Islam under very unfavourable conditions, and in an amazingly short time, without having undergone any previous training courses in teachers' colleges, or having studied the technical methods for teaching and stimulation. They learnt neither in military colleges nor in educational institutions. They came from the common people: merchants, craftsmen, and bedouin. They were able to spread Islam rapidly and effectively because of their firm faith and the force of Islam itself. They were the first generation of teachers in Islamic history.

Their first teacher was the Prophet (peace be upon him). Thereafter, they were taught by the Prophet's companions, then their successors and the Muslim *Ulama* how to seek guidance in the Quran, the sayings of the Prophet, al-Qiyas (judging matters in the light of Quran and the Prophet's sayings), and Muslims' consensus. They learnt how to utilize potential energies within themselves and in the Muslim *Ummah* for the benefit of the whole of mankind, and to kindle the sacred fire of faith in the hearts of all those with whom they came into contact in peace or in war.

Some individuals were undoubtedly devoted to teaching, especially to instructing children. Their number multiplied rapidly in the first few centuries of Islam, for several reasons:

(a) The Religion of Islam is optimistic as regards human destiny, and exhorts its followers to work for the future. So special care is taken to instruct children and young people, who represent the future.

(b) Islam makes it obligatory for every Muslim, male and female alike, to acquire education and to learn.

(c) Acceptance of Islam by great numbers of people made it necessary to give guidance to adults and to instruct the children, thereby inculcating the principles of Islam in their minds, and making it govern their thought and behaviour.

The high respect Islam accords to teachers shows clearly its recognition

142

of their vital role in educating and producing virtuous generations of Muslims and advancing Islamic society.

The men and women who gave guidance and instruction to Muslims from the very dawn of Islam came from among various social classes and chose the career which had been honoured by the Prophet's saying, 'I have been sent to be a Teacher', and his saying, 'I have been sent to complete good morality'. The Prophet himself (peace be upon him) used to teach at his mosque in Medina helped by some of his companions. He used to begin his instruction in the afternoon and to devote one day each week to women. After his death some of his companions followed his example. While sending a *Wali* (a governor) to a region that had accepted Islam, he used to send with him another person from his companions to teach the inhabitants of the region and instruct them in the faith of Islam.

In the early stage of Islam, there were three classes of teachers:

(i)   The Prophet's companions, their successors and the Ulema. They were not full-time teachers. They taught because it was incumbent upon the one who had knowledge to teach others in accordance with the instruction of Islam. At the same time, they performed other tasks and responsibilities.

(ii) A second class which devoted the greater part of its time to teaching. Religious chroniclers came into this class. As a rule, recruits came from among the less affluent Muslims; however, they had professions other than education to pursue because a learner was not expected to pay his instructor for his tuition.

(iii) The third class consisted of men who instructed and trained children. They usually came from among the poorer classes and the captives. Some had other professions whereby to earn a living, while Baitul-mal (the Public Treasury) secured a decent living for the rest.

Teachers usually taught in mosques where they used to sit with their students in circles. But after the first century of Hijra, education began to be organized in special places and *Kuttabs* (institutions for primary and religious education). Higher schools in the conventional sense did not appear until the fourth century A.H.

Children used to write on slates (made of stone, wood or bone) or on palm leaves, and to memorize passages from the Quran and Hadith. On the other hand, the grown-ups sat in circles round their teachers in mosques, madrassas, libraries, and 'ulama's houses, and read from a text book. A monitor would first read a passage aloud, and then the teacher would comment on it, explaining grammatical points, and describing places, names of tribes, their genealogy, deeds, and achievements in Islamic conquests. Then, he would proceed to expound the purpose of the passage, the religious teaching, the admonition etc. contained in it. This method of handling one book or one chapter at a time, and focussing attention on it and studying it from all aspects —linguistic, literary, historical, religious, and moral — and deducing every practical advantage from it, is valid and effective for the purpose of modern education.

The content of the subject-matter offered to students was taken mostly from the Quran, al-Hadith, religions, sciences, language, literature, history, genealogy, geography, and arithmetic.

The other branches of knowledge such as medicine, mathematics, astronomy, pharmacology and other sciences became a regular part of higher education during the Abbasid period at the turn of the 9th Century. The study of chemistry commenced earlier during the Omayyad period.

Qualified learners from different circles and centres of education were authorized to teach. The teachers, however, continued their training —especially because Islam had exhorted Muslims to pursue knowledge 'from cradle to grave' —by joining the teaching circles of renowned 'ulama, listening to speeches and poetry, and participating in the meetings of writers and contests of poets in seasonal fairs, and reading books. The number of books continued to increase and their prices became steadily lower because the number of copyists grew larger (al-Jahiz, the well-known writer was a copyist himself) and also because the Muslims produced cheap paper beginning from the third century A.H. (1). The system of Islamic education helped the teacher to make the best of his abilities and to educate his students in a balanced and successful way. It also helped him to adapt himself to his society and be an organic part of the Muslim *Ummah* in its march towards greater glory, deriving its power from faith and being guided by the light of Islam.

C. Teachers in the Near Past and the Present

Islamic education went on progressing during successive periods. Then it fluctuated in periods of prosperity and periods of decline, the latter being caused by the weakening of spiritual values, the disintegration of the Islamic *Ummah*, political and military disorders, and the weakening of the social and economic structure in most Muslim countries.

A number of factors brought about educational decay, the painful repercussions of which are being felt to this day:

(i) The Muslim mind lapsed into inertia and dropped creativity for imitation, and the substance for ephemeral appearances and style. In some Muslim countries, the purpose of education became the learning of texts by heart whether understood or not. Learners became content with the repetition of what older scholars had said, and confined their interest to interpreting a limited number of books and adding comments in the margins. Original and profound thought became rare, and very few would devote time to discovering the mysteries of nature or the laws of society which would contribute to its solidarity and prosperity, and which would help to disseminate the Islamic spirit and foster continued progress.

(ii) Another factor was the failure to promote technical and scientific knowledge although it flourished at one time in the Muslim world, and the renunciation of the branches of knowledge which were formerly studied by the Muslims, such as medicine, mathematics, chemistry and astronomy, on the erroneous assumption that they would lead to scepticism, uncertainty and unbelief.

(iii) Failure to educate women in a planned and regular manner as required by Islam.

(iv) Colonization, which came with the rise of the industrial power in the West, led to the subjugation of the Muslim world and other countries in Asia, Africa and America. One of the evils of political and military domination was that it deprived the Muslim world of free growth and independent life as required by Islam. The colonizer had no interest in religion (whether Islamic or Christian) except to manipulate it cunningly to further dominance over the conquered territories. The colonizer did all in his power to distort Islam in the eyes of Muslims and non-Muslims alike, and endeavoured to shake the Muslim's belief in their religion and to persuade them that their backwardness originated in the Islamic faith because it was rigid, uncompromising, and incompatible with modern civilization; that their salvation lay in adopting other religions, or in organizing their society on a rational and secular basis. This argument, supported by subtle psychological pressures and strengthened by the colonial system of education, had devastating effects on the Muslim community in Asia and Africa. Many among the rising generations of Muslims fell victim to alien ideologies, and several Muslim countries adopted a secular form of government and separated religion from politics. Some also secularized their educational systems, confining religious and spiritual education to the home and the mosque while public schools pursued physical and mental education, general culture and the teaching of professional skills. Islam, being a comprehensive religion, takes care of man as a whole —his spirit, mind, and body—at the same time. Education is deemed complete only when it takes into consideration the body, spirit, belief, worship, morals, knowledge, manual skills, and good manners as defined by Islam. The imposition of secularism on Islamic society is one of the worst afflictions that the colonizer brought about. It is a wound that is still hard to heal, because even now secularism finds some supporters among Muslims.

Despite all this, cultural colonization succeeded only partially because of the inherent strength of Islam and the steadfastness of the 'ulama and the Muslim teachers. But the enemy's failure to extinguish the light of Islam, and the 'ulama's and teachers' success in protecting it, could be only temporary. To make the success permanent, Muslims as a whole needed to know how to stick to their religion proudly and firmly, to defend it steadfastly and intelligently, and to adapt it to the current needs of the Islamic community. This task is long and formidable, and could be accomplished through the process of education. Muslim teachers need special qualifications and special training to enable them to meet the challenge.

At present, teachers come from among the poor classes because of the low salaries they receive, and most of them are employed by the government which supervises their selection, education, training and appointment to schools. Naturally, governments imposing secular education do not encourage teachers who advocate religious teaching in schools. It is necessary to bring about a change in national outlook if there is to be a change in the educational policy.

Today, in colleges of education or teachers' colleges, Muslim teachers receive an education that is alien in content, values, organization and objectives. The student teacher finds the teaching material instructive and modern, but it has no direct relation to his life; nor does it qualify him to understand and serve his community.

It was designed for a different type of student teacher in some Western country and was simply borrowed blindly. Besides, this material is completely divorced from religious teaching and the individual's spiritual development. The result is that student teachers, although they are Muslims, hardly attain sufficient knowledge of either Islamic or modern education and are consequently unable to show the relationship between modern knowledge and its educational principles or between Islamic knowledge and its educational basis.

Some of the basic assumptions underlying so-called 'modern' education or 'modern' programmes of teacher training are hardly valid as guides to human destiny. Only that which is scientific, technological, objective and rational is accepted as superior because it can be perceived by the senses and can be physically measured and verified. This school of thought regards intuition, sprirtual radiance and inner contemplation with suspicion, caution, and derision. Another assumption is that the training of man's mind is sufficient to ensure his full development and growth and that it would automatically guide his moral and social behaviour towards success. This attitude disregards the rich values which are latent in the human soul and are the only resource to bring about coherence in human personality and society. Values inherent in Islamic education promote religious life with its spiritual and moral concepts, inculcate noble feelings which accompany the transmission of a noble humanitarian message through teaching and instruction, and inspire to sacrifice for fellow human beings in order to win ultimately God's favour and reward.[2] A third assumption is that it is sufficient for the individual to obtain knowledge and information, which will then automatically create harmony in his mind and personality. This has proved to be mere wishful thinking. In fact unless man has an ideology to guide his steps, his mind becomes a storehouse of pieces of information, disorderly and uncreative, while his soul suffers from spiritual hunger and alienation.

Most modern teachers' colleges are planned on Western models. They produce teachers of preparatory, elementary or secondary schools, who become qualified to teach within the four walls of the schools but hardly fit to guide the community outside or to do anything substantial to improve society.

One of the main objectives of most teachers' colleges is to produce teachers for secular schools where religion is taught like an historical subject, or just as one subject among many others, and not as a subject superior to all others. The contemporary teacher of religion does not possess the status and influence which his predecessors used to possess. There are many other teachers alongside him who claim to be specialists. He is a civil servant. His freedom is limited, his salary is low, his income is small and his social contacts few because he is imprisoned in his school.

Today, those who discuss innovation in pedagogy and development of teachers' colleges, can be divided into three groups. One group is satisfied with imitating the old, another group, a comparatively small one, regards with admiration the gigantic rise of the West, its wealth and power, so it prefers to adopt the West's educational principles, ideas and methods as the model. The third group, which is the largest, is waiting to see educationists bring about reform, by co-ordinating Islamic education and Western education, by training teachers in such a way that they, together with their students, benefit from the inspiration of religion as well as the guidance of science; from the rules of moral conduct as well as the power of technology; and from the specialization of the scientist, and the comprehensive and broad outlook of the religious.

The First World Conference on Muslim Education was held to bring together eminent Muslim educationists, who looked deeply into the conflict between Islamic education and Western education and urged scholars to achieve a satisfactory solution for the future.

D. Developing Islamic Education for the Future

In my opinion such development should be on the following lines:

(a) *Winning the support of the Government.* The isolated individual or the devout hermit can live an Islamic life in isolation, but an Islamic society cannot be organized and Islamic education cannot be enforced without the approval and support of the Government. It is, therefore, necessary to convince the Government and eliminate all vestiges of hostility to the introduction of Islamic Education. Governments have often viewed religious and reform movements with scepticism because religious leaders were not always successful in keeping under control the behaviour of excited masses mobilized to support religion or reforms. Those devoted to serve Islam must be able to explain convincingly and demonstrate effectively to the people in power that the social, economic, educational and cultural advancement of a nation does not presuppose any hostility to religion, particularly when Islam lends strong support to continued progress of the *Ummah*. The jurisprudence of Islam is much ahead of its time since it is oriented to any eventualities which may arise in future.[3] The spiritual and moral power of Islam can help a Government to base its reforms on stabler foundations and to facilitate their enforcement.

The other factor is that reformers have relied on mobilizing the public to provide strong support without explaining their movement and their reforms to intellectuals, administrators, and influential persons, and without inviting these to support their cause by reasoned argument, thereby establishing a true dialogue in a civilized way as commanded by religion. Instead, the reformers regarded these as enemies from the start and confronted the government's organized power with the people's disorganized mutinies.

Any authority which succeeds in suppressing religious aspirations is a loser in the long run, because it has destroyed the major factor that consolidates a nation and protects it from disintegration. Also those religious movements which succeed in weakening state authority themselves become the losers.

(b) *Understanding Modern Western Civilization.* Modern Western civilization has merits and advantages which should not be denied or underrated. Its scientific and technological achievements and its process of research and discovery are not against the spirit of Islam, which enjoins exploration of everything unknown in the universe. Every new law discovered by man is considered a blessing given by God Almighty, who says 'We bestowed grace aforetime on David from Ourselves: "O ye mountains Sing ye back the praises of God with him! and ye birds also!' And we made the iron soft for him; — commanding: "Make thou coats of mail, balancing well the rings of chain armour, and work ye righteousness; for be sure I see all that ye do" ' (*Sura* XXXXiv).

On the other hand, Western civilization refuses to search for the primary causes and the Creator who is the origin of the universe.

Likewise it refuses to extend its gaze to the final outcome, the hereafter and the resurrection, because it cares only for the tangible and what can be measured or weighed. Everything which is beyond these limits is left to metaphysical studies.

Islamic education need not disapprove of everything in Western civilization but must continue to take cognizance of its shortcomings and failures, until it is fully established that the basic truths are no less important than other sciences in comprehending the secrets of the universe, human destiny, the relations between man and man, man and society, and man and his Creator. These truths are even richer food for thought, than other branches of knowledge. Islamic education must give them a degree of attention commensurate with their importance. The Muslim educationist will be able to elevate Islamic education to the level required in this age, if he takes part in the procedures of studying Western civilization, but recognizes its drawbacks in relation to Islamic thought.[4]

(c) *Safeguarding Man's Identity and Dignity.* Modern civilization, based as it is on enormous institutions and organizations, and industrial and technological establishments, has reduced 'Man' to an insignificant entity. It has dwarfed his personality out of all proportion and has impaired his dignity beyond recovery. He is enslaved to the enormous systems of modern civilization which continue to circumscribe his very existence and identity. Among the consequences of this loss of identity is that society has stripped the individual of most responsibilities. If he commits a crime his conduct is frequently attributed to heredity, temporary insanity, careless education on the part of parents, school or society, or to any other causes that relieve him of his responsibility and make him a dangerous and thoughtless machine. Conversely, in Islam man is put face to face with his responsibility, which is waived only in exceptional cases. According to the Quran: 'No bearer of burdens can bear the burden of another'. and 'Each individual is in pledge for his deeds'. 'He will have to give account of his deeds before the Lord, Islam establishes a strong link between freedom, dignity and responsibility'. 'Consequently, one of the most important points to attract the Muslim educator's attention is the development of human identity, individuality and responsibility.

(d) *Preparedness to face Future Challenges.* The anticipation of expected developments in human civilization is no less fruitful than studying its past stages and drawing lessons from its history. Futurology is the dominant theme of the present epoch calling for careful planning and

150

preparedness. It is incumbent upon Muslim scholars and educationists to study the trends, anticipate the challenges and be fully prepared to face them. It is obvious that man's command over nature and its laws will increase, and that he may even colonize the moon and the planets. In view of his developing capacities, which open up a series of alternatives before him, man will have to *choose* one of those alternatives to plan for the future of mankind. It will be a great misfortune for him if he fails to make the correct choice. Man's increasing command over nature through the ever larger orbit of his knowledge is in accordance with the spirit of Islam, so Islamic education should ensure full preparedness in facing the future with faith and confidence.

(e) *Making full use of each subject of research methods, and of modern teaching devices.* All subjects taught in schools provide occasion to think about the glory of God, and to reveal the amazing mysteries of nature and the secrets of life. A good teacher who understands his subject thoroughly is capable of conveying it to his students in an attractive way so that it is permeated with the spirit of Islam. Confining religious instruction to a few hours in the school curriculum has been a factor in weakening the religious spirit in some Muslim countries.

Workers for the promotion of religious education who would take advantage of various school activities should be aware of the urgent need for studies and research work on some important aspects of this approach such as the following:

(1) Studies are required in child and adolescent psychology to help develop the desired values and attitudes and resolve the conflicts arising out of the contradiction between ideal and reality, glorious past and present backwardness, conditions at home and conditions abroad. Conflicts also arise during the study of certain subjects when the content is not thoroughly discussed. Some subjects open the student's eyes to the omnipotence of God and the mysteries of the universe, to inspiring deep faith; others, such as the origins of the earth and of man, and the relationship between the body and the spirit, fill him with doubt and confusion, particularly when these subjects remain unexplained and obscure to him.

A comprehensive study of the crisis and the contradictory forces to which Muslim youth is exposed should be of great help to the teacher in understanding and guiding his students and inspiring confidence in them, to discover their individuality and strengthen their Islamic personality and identity. As the problem is a universal one, such a study should be undertaken in every Muslim country, so that a more comprehensive picture and more valid conclusions can be made available for the benefit of all. Such studies should be published in all the major languages of the Muslim world.

(2) There is an obvious need to acquaint both teachers and students with selected texts from the major Islamic classics which express the Islamic point of view on various educational issues. The imparting of Islamic education through chosen texts is one of the most interesting, efficient and effective methods for both teacher and student. These texts have to be crowned with some passages from the Quran, the traditions of the Prophet, and the sayings of the Prophet's companions, which indicate the merits of Islamic education and its originality. This collection of texts should then be published, so that it can serve as source material for Muslim educationists in writing the history of Islamic education, showing its merits, and producing more dependable data.

(3) The educational problems faced by the Islamic States need to be studied in depth in order to seek satisfactory solutions. Such study and research should deal with both theoretical and practical problems in all aspects of education. The majority of modern educational means and methods are not opposed to Islamic educational principles. Indeed, some of them have an Islamic origin, and some could be helpful in enriching the existing educational methods employed in Muslim countries. Among the more well-known methods of Islamic education are: (i) the organization of students into groups with monitors from amongst them to lead discussions; (ii) the presentation of the opponent's argument (truthful and complete) so that it can be clearly understood, followed by its refutation. (iii) The commitment of the student to self-education and life-long learning, which enables the teacher to guide his learning in accordance with his interest and ability, rather than to exercise compulsion and impose subjects on him. 'Self direction' becomes the mainstay of this method. (iv) the concentration of study on one single book which is made the starting point and centre of interest for further studies. This builds up a definite and firm basis for future development.

These methods, which originated in the theory and practice of Islamic education, have found acceptance even in some modern systems. However, modern psychology has lately been pressed into service for the development of such methods as indoctrination, subliminal perception, brain-washing, and the obliteration of some personality traits. These methods are not permitted by the teachings of Islam and cannot be practised in Muslim society. But they are becoming more varied and potent every day, which is a misfortune for mankind. The Muslim educator must be aware of them, so that he can reject them and take the necessary steps to have them banned. Islamic education naturally rejects these methods and refuses to employ them in the service of religion, because it believes in the dignity of man and protects him from being miseducated and misled.

The most effective way to produce and propagate good models of Islamic education would be to establish special Institutes of Education where qualified teachers-cum-educational leaders can be trained to demonstrate the theory and practice of Islamic education and to prepare more leaders in the field. I suggest that the first of these institutes should be established by King Abdulaziz University at the Mecca Campus.

To sum up: Islamic education has its own merits and characteristics, and it need not follow the example of other systems of education in order to attract attention or prove its worth.

In the past, the Islamic educational system has produced and developed societies with wide human horizons. After the general decline of the Islamic community, its educational institutions and their alumni (the 'ulama) were still a bulwark against its adversaries.

If Islamic education is to revive and resume the role it played in the past, it will have to reconsider the way teachers are trained and qualified, to infuse a religious spirit into every subject and course, to adopt suitable Islamic teaching methods, to organize student brotherhoods, to acquire the necessary techniques and skills for the advancement of society, to foster spiritual and moral values among both teachers and students, and to fill their hearts with the love of God and reliance on His support to serve Islam and humanity. For this purpose, model teacher training institutes should be established to demonstrate the immense potential of Islamic education and the relevance of its methods.

NOTES

1. Production of cheap paper was as important a factor in the diffusion of knowledge and education as the discovery of printing. In his book 'The Keys to Arabic Thought', Prof. V. Montei wrote: 'The battle of Talas was an era-making battle (751 A.D.). It took place on the borders of China, and Arabs learnt from Chinese prisoners-of-war the secret of paper manufacturing from hemp and flax. The first factory for making paper was established in Baghdad in the year 800 A.D. in the reign of Haroon er-Rashid and Charlemagne. Later, paper was carried to Europe by way of Muslim Spain in the twelfth century. The first paper factories were established in Italy and Germany in the fourteenth century of the Christian Era.'

2. In 1968 Western students revolted against their society and educational system. Their grievance against their ancestors was that the latter left them a society with endless wars, burdened with problems, and religious, national and racial strife; a society which suffered from an imbalance of wealth, prosperity and progress among nations and whose future seemed to be dark because nations continued to compete in the armaments race to increase their power of destruction instead of focussing their efforts on growth, peace, brotherhood, and human welfare. Their grievance against the educational system was that this did not prepare them for life in the right way but took care only of national thought and organization, and showed interest only in matters relating to science and technology. It failed to bring up individuals to love each other, to cooperate, to appreciate beauty, to give free play to imagination to observe the universe, to lift up their hearts to spiritual values, to develop the different aspects of man's personality and talents, respecting his humanity, dignity and freedom, and making him aware of his responsibilities before himself, his society, and mankind as a whole.

3. A French orientalist who studied very deeply the books of Ibn Taimiya declared: 'Islam has anticipated all modern systems in its labour laws.'

4. 'Islam is in its very nature a religion of struggle. From the day it first emerged it had to enter into ideological struggles in which it came out victorious. The ideological dangers surrounded it in the Abbasid Age, but it defeated them and left them behind. It was similarly triumphant in later conflicts. The present age is the age of the most violent ideological struggle throughout history. What Islam needs to come out victorious is not to introduce a new form of relationship between religion and life, but to be able to contain the ideologies of this age which form a challenge to it.' (Dr. Abul-Wafa et-Taftazani, *Alam al-Fikr*, 'The World of Thought', Vol. I, No. 1, Kuwait 1970).

Chapter Three

A System for the Preparation of Muslim Teachers

M. A. Ahmed Shami

Muhammad Ansar Ahmed Shami (b. 1937). He has been Associate Professor, King Abdulaziz University, Mecca, since 1976. He received his Ph.D. at East Lansing (Michigan) U.S.A. 1968 and has specialized in Education. He has ten years' teaching experience including eight years as a researcher and teacher in the U.S.A. He has published more than ten papers in literary journals of the U.S.A.

Teacher training in most countries comprises course work and student teaching experience. There are areas where this whole process takes about nine months. In some advanced countries, subsequent to formal teacher training, inservice training is also provided, to enhance the professional capabilities of the teacher. The existing teacher training programmes are geared to help develop the mind and body only. Nowhere in these programmes does 'spiritual education' appear as a goal of education. In some Western countries attention is being given to moral education, but this again is taken in a secular context, i.e. moral education in this world only and excluding Almighty Allah and the Hereafter.

In most Muslim countries, models for teacher training are taken from the West. These models, whose effectiveness has been questioned even in a secular context, are totally inadequate for training Muslim teachers, who are responsible for the development of the soul as well as of the mind and body. Again the teacher training programme will not be effective unless a *complete system* for teacher preparation, which incorporates all the important elements, is designed and properly implemented. A holistic approach is necessary. Taking parts alone and dealing with them in isolation may result in a waste of effort, and even in frustration.

155

1. Admission Criteria

At present criteria for admission to an educational programme are related primarily to intellectual and physical abilities. In the case of prospective Muslim teachers, who will be responsible for developing something for which Almighty Allah sent his messengers, the criteria for admission to teacher-education programmes must, in addition, provide for moral and spiritual qualities —devotion to Islam, firm faith (*iman*), human sympathy, sense of equality and justice and moral integrity. These traits should be discerned in an individual who chooses to be a teacher.

2. Course Work

The programme of course work for the preparation of teachers can be formulated by a harmonious blend of courses rooted in the Islamic tradition and courses followed in some modern systems of education.

While courses in history and philosophy of education or in methodology for student teachers can be developed on the basis of the Islamic tradition, further research will be necessary for the preparation of a *Muslim* teacher. Answers will have to be found to such questions as what are the characteristics of a Muslim teacher? How can these characteristics be developed? What special methodologies are needed to develop the student spiritually? If we are to arrive at suitable courses, we need to identify more issues of this kind and seek guidance from the Holy Quran; Life of the Holy Prophet (peace be upon him) and his traditions, lives of the Companions of the Prophet, lives of great Muslims and our own experience.

The selection of courses from modern educational systems will be difficult. These courses will be mainly from such areas as educational psychology, methods of teaching, and measurement. But the contents of each course will have to be selected with reference to their established value and utility. Also, we shall need an ingenuity and competence if we are to blend these contents successfully with those of the Islamic tradition and relate them to our own community needs and environment. Depending upon the topic which is being introduced a teacher could relate its content to Islam in many ways. The only precondition is that the teacher should be a devoted Muslim and possess relevant knowledge of *din*.

3. Student-teaching

Student-teaching experience is provided under the guidance of experienced teachers, and the main objective of the programme is to help the student teacher to teach better. A Muslim student teacher should be expected to go beyond the teaching of a subject. He should be equally concerned with the improvement of student behaviour. To achieve this, he should himself manifest the behaviour expected of a good Muslim, including scholarship, initiative, observance of *ibādat*, respect for others' rights and property, courtesy, etc. These characteristics are even more important than the ability to teach well. We must evolve a model of student teaching which will completely meet our requirements.

The experienced teacher working with a student teacher must evaluate him on his teaching skills and, more important, on his effectiveness as a model of Muslim personality. The quality of his guidance should be imbued with the Islamic spirit.

4. Organizational climate

The most important quality of a Muslim teacher is not what he knows, but what he is. It is what people become that is important, and the organizational climate has a direct bearing on this. Therefore, the organizational climate for preparing Muslim teachers must be truly Islamic in character. In this climate, people help one another to avoid reprehensible action and encourage the performance of desirable actions. More specifically, the presence of an Islamic climate may be noticed and evaluated in terms of *ibādat* and *muamlāt*.

An institution which prepares Muslim teachers must provide suitable facilities and encourage the performance of *ibādat*. Time must be allocated for prayers, and the leaders of the institution must manifest strict adherence to the rules of *dīn* and join in the prayers of the congregation. Also the leaders of the institution must impart

Islamic teachings of *muamlāt* through their own exemplary behaviour in all aspects of human relations, both inside and outside the institution.

It is necessary for the domain of *muamlāt* to be further categorized and for plans to be made to influence the behaviour of all individuals. For example, the *muamlāt* may be classified in terms of interaction between students and students; students and teachers; teachers and teachers; teachers and administrators; students and administrators. The head of an institution may be considered as *ameer* and his role as an *ameer* should be clearly defined.

5. Voluntary Service

Like our bodies, the Spirit (*ruh*) also feeds on several things. Apart from *zikr* and *ibādat*, one of the most important nourishments for *ruh* is the service conducted voluntarily for others with the sincere intention of pleasing Almighty Allah and the Holy Prophet (peace be upon him). Although every Muslim needs continuous spiritual progress the growth of *ruh* for a teacher is more important. He is the one in whose hands we place our tender and innocent children. He possesses our trust. He has to stand at a higher level than an average individual so as to feed the minds and hearts of our children. He has to be a person who is on the job not during school hours only but all the time. He has to shed light wherever he is.

One way for developing such an individual is to inculcate in him the habit of voluntary service. In teacher preparation programmes, the institution should persuade its student teachers to select and organize any voluntary service they would like to undertake. For example, they may tutor poor students, organize youth activities, participate in community development, or they may conduct activities for *tableegh* or *dīn*. To be able to persuade their students to perform voluntary service, the staff of the teacher-preparation institutions must themselves be involved in voluntary service. They must be models for their students.

6. Evaluation of student-teachers

If we accept that the most important thing for the Muslim teacher is not what he knows but what he is, then logically the evaluation of 'what he is' becomes more important than 'what he knows'. However, it is more difficult to evaluate 'what a person is' than 'what he knows'. We will need to develop a comprehensive model for this type of evaluation. Also the evaluation has to be continuous to help student teachers improve themselves, both academically and behaviourally. Although after proper selection procedures, meticulous training, exemplary behaviour by the staff and the voluntary service programme, many students will be fit to become teachers, graduation from a teacher-preparation institution should not be automatic. At the conclusion of the preparatory programme, the data about academic performance, behaviour patterns, and previous evaluation of each student should be reviewed. Giving priority to qualitative behaviour over academic performance, decisions should be taken to retain a student or to let him graduate.

7. In-Service education

Graduation from a teacher-preparing institute should not mean that a person would not need further improvement. Rather graduation should be considered as an entry permit into a field where a person has to attain continuous growth and development. Islam enjoins continuous growth and life-long education. Therefore, during the early stages of a teacher's service he should be placed with a Guide teacher who can help him to solve his problems and to progress further. Not only the new teacher or the guide teacher but the whole school should have a constant inward look and be continuously searching for self-renewal. Professional enhancement and spiritual elevation can always find room for development in every person at any age and at any time. This is a lesson provided by our *dīn*, that there is no end to one's progress and improvement.

To sum up, the teacher-preparation programmes for Muslim teachers should not be a carbon copy of the programmes in the West or anywhere else. Muslim teachers, in addition to caring for the minds and bodies of their students, are also responsible for inspiring their

159

souls. Consequently, teacher-preparation programmes for Muslim teachers must respond to this additional responsibility by including additional courses, establishing a conducive organizational climate, modifying student-teaching practices, organizing voluntary services and implementing proper evaluation and in-service programmes.

Chapter Four

Reconstruction of Teacher Education in Islamic Society

N. A. Baloch

Nabi Ahmed Baloch was born in 1917 in Sind (Pakistan). He is Secretary, Ministry of Education, Government of Pakistan. His degrees include B.A. (Hons), University of Bombay, India; M.A. LL.B Aligarth Muslim University, India; M.A., Ed.D., Columbia University, U.S.A. He was Professor of Education in Sind University from 1950 to 1972 and has been Professor Emeritus since then; he was also Vice-Chancellor, University of Sind 1973–1976. He is the author/editor of some fifty publications and has participated in many international conferences and seminars.

Before presenting my views on the reconstruction of teacher education in Islamic society, I wish to make it clear that these views are strictly personal, in the sense that they are based upon a partial understanding of 'Islam' (as given in the infinitely meaningful concept *Inn al-Dīn inda-Allah al-Islam*) and of the model way of life of the Islamic community (as comprehended in the concept of *al-Shariat al-Islmiyyah*). Also I am not attempting to present a 'model scheme' of teacher education; I am more concerned to delineate the process whereby such a scheme can be formulated. These views, presented without any intention or claim that they represent what is the best or the most authentic, demonstrate just one way of thinking about the subject, and any one exposition of views always presupposes a better exposition (*fauq kull dhi'ilm 'alim*).

Studies Needed to Formulate a Valid Programme of Teacher Education

Since the education of teachers is an inseparable and integral part of Islamic education, its basic objectives remain the same as those of Islamic education. To formulate a valid programme of teacher education in a Muslim society (country), studies are needed (i) to define the more specific requirements of Islamic education and develop some Guiding Principles which may serve as the main directional goals for the whole system, including teacher education; and (ii) to determine the implications of the Guiding Principles in the light of the actual needs and problems of each country and its local conditions, so that a sound and beneficial programme of education can be developed. Currently, the need for survival, identity, independence and progress is keenly felt in all Muslim countries. Among their most pressing problems are: imparting the right type of education to their young, promoting economic development, improving community health and sanitation, and developing competence for co-operative action to manage the affairs of the community and the country. Islamic education in general, and teacher education in particular, are related to the solution of all these important problems, particularly the most pressing ones.

Formulating the Guiding Principles

The Holy Quran has established the superiority of 'knowledge' and urged man to learn and to educate himself, and to continue to think over and study the entire creation—all that pertains to 'man' (*al-Nās/anfusihim*) and the rest of the Universe (*al-āfāq/al-ard wa al-samāvāt*)—so that he can understand the nature and the process of creation. He can thus be led to the realization of the One Supreme Creator of all, through the discovery of the Final Truth and the Ultimate Reality of the Universal Laws of God (*al-āyāt*) operating in the universe as the manifestation of His Absolute Will. Also, with his advancing knowledge and firm faith in the One Supreme Creator of all, man can establish an 'Islamic Society' which is based on peace (*an-amn wa al-salām*), truth (*al-haqq*), excellence (*al-khair*), beauty (*al-hasnat*), justice

162

and equity (*al-'adl wa al-ihsan*) so that it becomes a 'model' for mankind to follow (*ummatan wasatan li-takunu Shuhada ala al-nās*). The development of a 'model society' will call for the judicious and righteous application of accumulating knowledge and understanding to the changing needs and problems of society at different times and under different conditions, so that by continuous modelling and improvement it will evolve as 'the very best model' (*Khair Ummah*).

In accordance with the above concepts, education in a Muslim society, to be truly Islamic in character, must have among others the following main guiding principles:

(a) To promote the acquisition of more and more new knowledge skills, insights and understandings, and to motivate the search and the research required to know the unknown (*ma lam ya'lam*), the ultimate reality behind all things (*Allāhumma'arinī haqāiq' al-ashyā' kamā hiya*) and, thus to discover the eternal laws of Allah operating throughout the entire creation in order to know Him as the One Supreme Creator of all. The learning process must commence with the learner's faith in the Creator (*Iqra' bi ism rabbika alladhī khalaq*) and continue to confirm and consolidate his faith in the Creator to the very end (*hattā ya'tiyaka al-yaqīn*).

(b) To motivate the righteous and judicious use of knowledge (i) for the exemplary development of an individual's conduct and character, and (ii) for devising a practical programme of action (*al-Iamal al-Salih*) to improve a particular Muslim society as well as the whole Islamic Community (*Ummah*) and thus enable it to continue its progress towards higher stages of development.

Application of the Guiding Principles and a General Strategy for Action

The strategy for applying the Guiding Principles to the educational system requires a clear vision of their implications so as to determine the more specific 'teaching-learning objectives' which should be achieved at different levels of education. These are the specific 'achievement goals' which should guide the actual educative process in terms of quality, quantity and direction. The main responsibility for developing this strategy lies with the teacher.

In view of their implications, the two 'Guiding Principles' can be restated in the form of specific 'achievement goals', as follows:

The first principle implies:

1. Commencing the educative process with faith in the one Supreme Creator of all and confirming and consolidating one's faith continuously to the very end.
2. Acquiring more and more 'new' knowledge in terms of information, facts, skills, understanding and insight.
3. Studying Man and all that concerns him, particularly his role as a 'Muslim'.
4. Studying the Universe in all its aspects.
5. Continuing the process of search and research so as to discover the ultimate truth and reality of the Laws of God which operate in the world of Man and in the rest of the Universe.

The second principle implies:

6. Integrating faith and knowledge, in terms of their implication and application.
7. Improving oneself so as to become a useful member of the family, society, and the Islamic Community (*Ummah*).
8. Engaging in productive work for lawful gain (*Kasb al-Halal*) in order to be able to contribute to the well-being of the family, community and country.
9. Studying and identifying the needs and problems of society.
10. Participating in constructive programmes of action (*al-amal al-salih*) to contribute one's best to the improvement of society.
11. Developing specific abilities, skills and understanding in order to be able to contribute effectively to the most pressing problems of society, such as educational advancement, economic development, health improvement, and cooperative community action; thus to be able to govern the country and safeguard independence.
12. Developing and using the country's resources, both human and material, for the continuous improvement of society.

Such 'achievement goals' for pupils will have a direct bearing on the preparation of teachers.

Defining the Purposes and Policies for Teacher Education

It is essential that the three previous studies should be undertaken as necessary pre-requisites for the reconstruction of teacher education in Muslim society. It is on the basis of such studies that the purposes and policies for the recruitment, education, employment, and assessment of teachers' work should be defined by each Muslim country.

As a general guideline, *the preparation of teachers is to be directly related to the educational objectives to be achieved in the light of the basic 'Guiding Principles' and the 'specific achievement goals' set for different levels of learning.* The main purpose of teacher education is, obviously to produce 'good teachers', but this is not enough by itself. It becomes necessary to formulate policies which, by minimizing the problems and extending the essential facilities, create an environment which enables the 'good teacher' to contribute his very best towards the achievement of educational goals. In an Islamic educational system, the community is directly responsible for creating such conditions. The concept of the 'good teacher' and the 'purposes and policies' of teacher education may vary in different Muslim countries in terms of their own 'Guiding Principles' and their 'specific achievement objectives', and in accordance with their own needs, problems and conditions.

It is, however, necessary that a Muslim country should have a clear concept of 'excellence' for its own teachers. To be able to visualize the distinctive role of the teacher in a given Muslim society, there is a question that can be asked in a wider context: How does 'excellence in a teacher' in a Muslim society differ from 'excellence in a teacher' in any other society? One way to answer this question is as follows:

The teacher in a Muslim society excels to the extent that he succeeds in educating a pupil so that, according to his level of maturity, the pupil:

(a) develops faith in the One Supreme Creator of all;
(b) acquires the kind of knowledge and understanding which enable him to think and to develop a spirit of inquiry in order to discover the laws of the Supreme Creator operating in the universe;
(c) is motivated to use his knowledge, skills, and understanding to improve himself and society.

165

The purpose and policies of teacher education are to be defined by each Muslim society, but these must concentrate on producing the type of 'good teacher' whose 'excellence' is measured in terms of his/ her faith and belief, personal qualities of conduct and character, professional competence and actual achievement in terms of his above-mentioned contribution.

With these preliminaries stated, a set of criteria can now be put forward for the recruitment, education, employment and assessment of teachers' work in a Muslim society. It should be made clear, however, that this list is not an exhaustive one, nor is the formulation of each criterion a final one. These criteria are proposed in order to stimulate thinking and to call attention to some of the basic requirements of teacher education in a Muslim society.

These criteria should be adopted as 'policy decisions' in order to give a focus and direction to the programme of teacher education in a Muslim country. It is necessary, too, that the 'criteria' and the 'Policy Decisions' should emerge from the basic convictions and consensus of society rather than that they should be adopted or imposed as administrative measures on the basis of expediency. Therefore, in the following pages, the criteria are stated in the form of 'beliefs' and 'convictions' of Muslim society. For a programme of action, these are to be translated into 'policy decisions' which should represent 'convictions' and 'commitments' of a Muslim society in the field of teacher education. It can be substantiated that historically, the best of the Muslim educational thinking has been on these lines.

I. *Muslim society should Ensure a Full Complement of Good Teachers Within its Educational System*

This conviction arises from the commandment (*'iqra''*) and the concepts (e.g. *hal yastavī al-lādhiñ ya'lamūn wa al-ladhīn la ya'lamūn*) of the Holy Quran and the guidance of the Holy Prophet (sal'm) (*al-'ilm faridatun alā kull muslimin,,* and also *utlibu al-'ilm . . .*) which enjoin the 'seeking of knowledge and learning' as an obligatory duty for every member of Muslim society. Consequently, it becomes an obligatory duty for the Muslim community to provide teachers and facilities for teaching. Also the commandments of the Holy Quran and the traditions of the Prophet regarding the acquisition of knowledge require that a foundation programme of universal, free, compulsory elementary education should be instituted to guarantee the minimum necessary education for all. In addition, opportunities for further education should be provided, particularly in those fields of knowledge which are considered essential for the advancement of Muslim society. To meet these objectives the supply of teachers becomes obligatory. This calls for a policy decision in a Muslim country that all necessary steps should be taken to ensure that good teachers become available for the foundation programme of universal, free, compulsory education, and for such other levels and in such areas of study as are considered to be a necessary part of the system.

II. *Muslim society believes in the worth of the Teacher and recognizes his/her Special Role and Status in the Educational System and in Society*

This conviction arises for the highest role of those who 'know and teach', as underlined in the Holy Quran and in the tradition of the Holy Prophet (sal'm). The position of those 'who know and are righteous' is only next to that of the Prophets. They are to be consulted and they are capable of giving the best guidance. The Prophet (sal'm) is reported to have said that human beings who count belong to one of the two categories, the teachers and the learners, the rest being a mere rabble. Since an Islamic society can be sustained and advanced only on the basis of Faith, Knowledge and Education, the role of the teacher assumes the highest importance both in the educational system and in society. It is a hall-mark of Muslim society that it has the best teachers.

Thus the special role and status of the teacher should be recognized officially in the educational system and in society. The nature of his/ her social and professional recognition in terms of remuneration and rewards, both in cash and in kind, must be determined by each society but it has to be guaranteed as a matter of policy. This will not only ensure a supply of good teachers for all levels of education, but will also be an indispensable investment in human resources.

III. *Muslim society recognizes that formulating the curriculum, planning and conducting the teaching-learning procedures, certifying student accomplishment, and managing and directing educational institutions are essentially the privilege and the responsibility of the teacher.*

This conviction arises out of the implications of the first two criteria underlining the worth and work of the teacher, and is confirmed by the consensus of the Islamic community throughout history. The function of teaching and educating in Islamic society has been essentially the prerogative of the teacher, and even the most powerful kings and the mightiest emperors have recognized this. Historically speaking, education in Muslim society has been essentially teacher-managed and community-supported. Even when the State financed and founded education, educational institutions appeared on the initiative of the great Prime Minister, Nizamul Mulk (d. 485), and later under Nuruddin (d. 569) and the Ayubids, they were managed by the teachers. Even when teachers were invited and honoured with appointments, there was no interference with their work. Managing and directing the institutions, planning the teaching procedures, recommending books for study and finally certifying a student's accomplishment on the basis of direct *al-Sama'*, or confirming his competence by *al-Ijāzah*, were the direct responsibilities of the teachers.

New policies, therefore, need to be agreed for the reconstruction of teacher education on the basis of this sound practice which developed early in Islamic society. The present policies, arising out of borrowed models, have projected 'administrative authority' to such an extent that it has seriously curtailed the initiative, dignity and freedom of the teacher. This has been done by bringing in the 'specialist' and different types of Special Committees, instituting external examinations to evaluate student performance, and extending the administrator's discretion and decision-making power in the actual management and direction of educational institutions. Wherever such measures have been in force, the teacher's initiative, performance and sense of responsibility have been seriously impaired.

IV. *Muslim society believes that the Teacher in the Islamic Educational System is a 'committed teacher' and therefore, balances his special responsibility with his accountability*

This conviction arises out of the basic consideration that as learning is an obligatory duty, teaching, too, is an obligatory responsibility. The early Muslim community considered teaching almost a sacred and religious obligation, which was to be fulfilled by every qualified member of the Muslim community as a free service, without accepting any remuneration. The example was set by the Holy Prophet (sal'm), the four Caliphs and their contemporaries. In principle, the Prophet (sal'm) approved payment for teaching, but in fact only non-Muslim teachers were remunerated, and Muslim teachers provided a free service for the sake of Allah, their efforts contributing to the very survival and advancement of the Islamic community. Thus a Muslim teacher became committed to the spread of knowledge and to consolidating the foundations of Faith.

Later, the Muslim community began to contribute to the maintenance and welfare of the teacher, but even after Muslim teachers were handsomely paid (particularly following the establishment of the State institutions in the 5th and 6th century), the principle of dedication and commitment on the part of teacher to consolidate the faith and to spread knowledge was firmly established and was recognized by both teacher and the community.

Secondly, the new dispensation under Islam which made learning obligatory for every Muslim also implied that every human child had the capacity to learn. Not only was the teacher committed to teach him/her but he was to teach him/her in a way that he/she learnt according to his/her own ability and level of maturity.

For these reasons, but mainly because of the inseparable bond between 'Islam' and 'education', the teacher in Muslim society has to be a 'committed' teacher, and consequently 'accountable' to society.

In this context, a teacher's harsh treatment of a child was quick to attract attention and the great educators like al-Ghazali (*Ihyā' Ulūm al-dīn*) and ibn Miskwaih (*Tahdhib al-Akhlaq*) advocated the use of rewards, recognition and recreation (play) by the teacher to motivate learning, rather than any form of punishment. Ibn Khaldun explained how capital punishment was psychologically harmful and distorted the normal growth and development of the child. At the same time as these views were expressed, teachers' accountability also came under

169

juridical definition within the general subject of *al-Hisbah*, and the concept of 'accountability' was extended particularly to the entire work and methodology of the elementary teacher and his treatment of children. Al-Shaizari (d. 589 H.), Ibn Bassām (following al-Shaizari), Ibn al-Akhywwah (d. 729 H.) and others in their works discussed '*al-hisbah 'alā mu'addabi al-sibyan*' in detail.

The above concepts imply that a teacher in Muslim society is not a mere wage earner or professional worker (as he is supposed to be in some modern educational systems), but a specially commissioned and committed member of society, and that in view of his high status and special responsibility, he has to be 'accountable' to society in the discharge of his duties. This has been one of the unique contributions of Muslim educational thought to the theory and practice of education, and it should form the basis of any 'policy decision' that is taken for the reconstruction of teacher education.

V. *Muslim society believes that the worth of a teacher lies both in his personal accomplishments and in his professional competence.*

This conviction arises from the basic concepts embodied in the Guiding Principles according to which the pursuit of knowledge is not enjoyed for knowledge's sake, but for establishing the truth, for knowing the Creator, and for improving and developing a 'model' Islamic society. These become the foremost objectives to be promoted by the teacher: he has to impart knowledge and simultaneously he has to contribute to the wholesome development of the learner to enable him to seek truth, and to improve his own self and society. As such, a teacher's personal qualities of conduct, character and scholarship are as important as his professional competence to be able to impart instruction effectively in terms of faith, knowledge, skills and under-standing required at any given level. This implies that in a Muslim society it is not enough that a teacher should know the subject and should be able to teach it: the necessary pre-requisite for teaching is to establish what type of person he is —i.e. his own personal worth in terms of faith and conduct and his ability to guide the young to grow and develop as committed members of Muslim society. This criterion must become the guiding principle for the recruitment and appoint-ment of teachers in a Muslim country. It has a direct bearing, too, on the curriculum for the education of teachers, which will be discussed later.

VI. *Muslim society believes in the life-long work and competence of the teacher, maintains him accordingly and provides him with continued opportunities to advance himself in knowledge and understanding for the continuous improvement of his teaching procedures and the better guidance of the young, as well as for his self-improvement and better service to society.*

This conviction arises out of the concept of life-long education commended by the Holy Prophet (*Utlibū al-'ilm min al-mahd ilā al-lahd*). 'Learning' and 'Teaching' being obligatory functions, a Muslim must continue to learn and be prepared to teach what he knows, throughout his life. The learning and teaching process should continue even after the formal period of schooling. This underlines the importance of the life-long role of the teacher. Having a special responsibility and status and being 'committed' and 'accountable', a teacher in Muslim society becomes a 'precious asset' to be conserved for life-long service to society. He is not just an employee who serves for a specific period and then retires; he never retires and is not retired. He continues to teach and guide unless there are any compelling circumstances which force him not to do so; or until he becomes physically handicapped or too feeble to teach because of his age. In view of his life-long work and the increasing demands on his competence, he is to be given continued opportunities to advance himself in knowledge, which keeps advancing at the same time. Even when he becomes feeble or physically handicapped, he is to be maintained and looked after properly by society.

These six criteria derive their worth and validity both from the teachings of Islam as well as from educational thought in early Muslim society. These and any other criteria of a similar nature ought to be the corner-stones for the new structure of teacher education in a Muslim country. They have definite implications for the organization of institutions as well as for the curriculum for the education of teachers.

The Need for a New Type of Broad-based Integrated Institution

Under the Islamic educational system, purposeful broad-based education takes precedence over specialization, particularly in the case of the teacher. The teacher in Muslim society is not a narrow specialist or a technician to be trained in a separate institution. Therefore, no separate institutions were established for the training of teachers. A teacher was not being 'trained' but he was being 'educated'; he was not being 'isolated' but 'associated'. *Murāfiqah* or 'associated learning', particularly emphasized by the Shafa'ite school of thought, envisaged the development of social intelligence in the student so that he could become an efficient member of the Islamic community. It can be inferred that the theory and practice of education in early Muslim society was orientated more towards the development of a teacher as an enlightened guide, or (using the modern terminology) a 'social scientist', in so far as his professional work was concerned. All students grew up both as 'learners' and 'teachers' in their own spheres of work and, as such, all were educated together. Thus, the teacher was educated at the same time as he learned to teach. Individual attention by the teacher, individual presentation and exposition by each student in the *halqa* after the teacher had introduced the subject, the practices and procedures of *murafiqah* and *munazirah*, and the institution of *Muīd*—all contributed to the development of 'a teacher' in the maturing student.

This is a distinctive contribution of Muslim educational thought and practice, the importance of which has come to be recognized in the new trends in some modern educational sytems, in which the training of teachers was for long advocated as a 'specialization' to be accomplished in 'separate'institutions. This narrow concept of 'training' teachers in separate institutions and in isolation, is now giving way to more integrated and broad-based institutions, and this trend in the U.S.A. would seem to have contributed to the 'demise of separation in teacher education'.[1] In the U.S.S.R., there are special Pedagogical Institutes, but these are highly developed university type institutions.

There is, obviously, a need for the development of a new type of broad-based institution which provides for integrated programmes of education whereby students intending to become 'teachers within the

172

educational system' continue to follow common studies along with their fellow students, but undertake additional studies and also receive special guidance which will contribute to their self-development and professional competence as teachers.

This concept of an integrated programme of education for the teacher also implies that all prospective teachers will be educated in the same institution. There is to be no disparity between this system and those current systems involving separate institutions for the training of elementary and secondary teachers.

In Muslim society, the 'integrated whole education' of teachers takes precedence over the limited concept of 'training'. The preparation of teachers in separate training insitutions or the training of different types of teachers in separate institutions does not therefore conform to the spirit of Islamic education. The teacher in Muslim society should be educated to lead and guide the younger generations rather than be trained to become a master of methods and techniques of teaching. This brings us to a consideration of the curriculum for the education of teachers.

The Curriculum Guidelines For Teacher Education

Some conclusions regarding the nature of the curriculum for the education of teachers can be drawn from what has been said so far.

Firstly, as a general guideline, the education of teachers should be directly related to the educational objectives to be achieved in the light of the basic 'Guiding Principles' and the specific 'achievement goals' which are set for the different levels of education in the System. The implications of the Guiding Principles in terms of the specific 'achievement goals' have already been given in some detail.

Secondly, in view of the special role and status of the teaching profession (*Criteria II*), the curriculum for teacher education is to be geared to the preparation of teachers who are 'committed' and 'accountable' in terms of their work and responsibility.

Thirdly, the curriculum for the education of teachers must simultaneously aim at the development of *both* their personal accomplishment as good Muslims and their professional competence (*Criteria IV*). Professional competence will include the teacher's ability, understanding and initiative to plan curriculum, organize teaching procedures, assess student accomplishment, and manage the educational institution (*Criteria III*).

This curriculum will need constant thought, continued adjustments in the light of experience, and concerted efforts to develop it in order to produce the type of teachers needed by Muslim society. The need for an integrated, objectives-orientated and purposeful education has already been underlined. Modern systems, from which the Muslim countries keep borrowing, have gone for 'differentiation' of educational curricula, including those of Teacher Education for individual adjustment and further specialization. While 'differentiation' has served a purpose by meeting individual needs in those systems where 'individual' takes precedence over the 'community' and 'specialization' is more in fashion, it has also promoted compartmentalization and even disparities. Some of the modern systems have accepted the trinity of 'General', 'Special' and 'Professional' as being the main components of teacher education. The principle of integration which derives its strength and validity from the concept of *'al-Tawhid'*, has to be accepted as the operative principle at all stages and in all aspects of Islamic Education, including the curriculum for teacher education.

translated from Arabic by
S. Khokhar

NOTES

1. In his paper on 'Teacher Education in the United States' prepared for the UNESCO Expert Committee on Teacher Education (Paris, 4–15 Dec., 1967), Dr. Robert J. Schaefer, Dean of the Teachers College, Columbia University, New York, confirmed what he then called the 'demise of separation in teacher education' in the U.S.A.

Chapter Five

The Role of Faculties of Education in Teacher-Training
The Kingdom of Saudi Arabia: A Case Study

M. Al-Ahmad Al-Rasheed
A. R. Abdul-Latif

Muhammad Al-Ahmad Al-Rasheed has the following degrees: B.A. (Riyadh), M.A. in Educational Administration (Indiana), Ph.D. in Administration of Higher Education (Oklahoma). He is a Saudi and was formerly Dean of the Faculty of Education, University of Riyadh. He is a member of the American Association for Higher Education and participated in the Conference on Higher Education, Chicago 1396 A.H. He has participated in several other conferences and his publications include a number of books and papers on Education.

Ahmed Rifat Abdul-Latif. It is regretted that at the time of publication Dr Ahmed Rifat Abdul-Latif's biographical details were not available.

Introduction

It is a universally acknowledged truth that the growth of contemporary societies, developed or developing, does not take place either haphazardly or along unintended lines. On the contrary, short and long term plans are carefully premeditated and carried out before any substantial growth is foreseeable. In other words, we can safely say that social change is not an end in itself. What is more significant is the purposeful change which drives man in society towards a better position in all walks of life.

175

Hence planning for change has become one of the distinctive features of man's intellectual and practical activities, and it occupies a prominent place in all countries and educational institutions whatever social and political ideologies these countries adopt. It has also become a remarkably extensive field for researchers in economics and behavioural sciences. Efforts made in these areas usually come under the heading of 'development'.

As a sociological concept, social development is sometimes misinterpreted, particularly when more attention is focussed on economic and material aspects of society in an attempt to increase national production and raise national revenue. The sub-division of development into economic and social development may be justifiable within the sphere of abstract thinking and theoretical speculation which aim at minimizing prevailing social problems. But in the actual process of development such intellectual duality does not discernibly exist. We can very easily distinguish between problems closely linked with either aspect of development, social or economic. But this artificial distinction does not mean that the two aspects of development are separable or not interdependent. They reflect the two sides of the same coin. Economic development cannot be achieved in the absence of a corresponding development of those human resources engaged in the field of national production and public utilities.

In the light of innumerable investigations carried out in this area, we can safely say that economic development is closely associated with and dependent upon the efforts and contributions made in the field of social development, particularly those aiming at producing qualitatively and quantitively skilful and educated manpower required for development plans.[1]

Studies were made to find out why, in some countries, some particular development plans had failed to achieve the set objectives. The results of these studies attributed this failure to insufficiency of manpower and to the ineffectiveness of human investment in the field of education.[2]

The Situation of the Saudi Teacher

The Kingdom of Saudi Arabia attaches considerable importance to all educational matters in the belief that education is the central core in any comprehensive development plan. This is unmistakably seen in the ever-increasing budgets assigned to education in the Ministry of

Education and Higher Education, and the General Administration for the Education of Girls as well as other ministries which organize and finance educational programmes for their employees. The Kingdom is sparing no effort to promote and secure general education, in all stages, for boys and girls, to cater for technical education, to increase the number of universities and higher education colleges, and to send more graduates to carry on post-graduate studies abroad. The ever-growing importance the government attaches to education, is reflected in several remarkable achievements. Many schools and educational institutions have been established and equipped with the latest scientific and technological apparatus and appliances, as well as with modern means of education. The curricula of education have been further developed and the latest teaching methods and means of evaluation introduced.

Yet, we do believe that such achievements in the field of education cannot be fruitful until the country has trained and made available efficient teachers who can undertake and shoulder the responsibility of teaching future generations to the best of their ability. In this study we have concentrated, more than anything else, on the present situation of the Saudi teacher and the role of colleges of education in teacher training. We shall focus on training intermediate and secondary school teachers since this is the main function of colleges of education.

The Shortage of Saudi Teachers

It is quite obvious that the enormous increase in the number of schools and students throughout the Kingdom has outpaced the increase in the number of Saudi teachers. The latest statistics show that the number of Saudi teachers in secondary, intermediate and teacher-training institutes bears no relation to the number of students enrolled in these schools, or to the number of students enrolled in these schools, or to the number of non-Saudi teachers on contract with the Ministry of Education and the General Administration for the Education of Girls. The following statistical tables reveal this phenomenon:

(1) *In the Intermediate Stage*

This table shows clearly the total number of teachers in the intermediate stage and the ratio of Saudi to non-Saudi teachers in the course of two successive years.

Table 1

Distribution of teachers in intermediate schools and the percentage of Saudi teachers to the total number of teachers in this stage, in accordance with the subjects taught in 1394/95 and 1395/96 A.H.

Subject	1394/95 A.H.			1395/96 A.H.			% of Rise or Fall
	Total Number	Number of Saudis	% of Saudis to Total Number	Total Number	Number of Saudis	% Saudis to Total Number	
Religion	959	702	73	1087	38·7	35·6	37·4 −
Arabic Language	770	294	38	843	255	30·3	7·7 −
Arabic & Religion	56	20	35·7	69	16	13·2	12·5 −
English	747	38	5	934	85	9·1	4·1 +
Social Sciences	569	320	56	660	372	56·4	·4 +
Maths	542	58	10·7	688	79	11·5	·8 +
Physical Sciences	453	92	20	775	105	18·3	1·7 +
Science & Maths	146	11	7·5	117	6	5·1	2·4 −
Physical Education	279	92	33	319	86	27	6·0 −
Art Education	372	131	35	424	110	26	·9 −
Vocational Subjects	19	10	53	21	14	66·7	13·7 +
	4912	1768	36	5737	1515	26·4	9·6 −

178

Statistical data mentioned in Table I are quoted from:
(1) Ministry of Education: *Efficiency Level of Teachers in General Education Stages &*
Teacher-Training Institutes in 1394/95 A.H., Page 13.
(2) Ministry of Education: *Statistical Diary of 1395/6 A.H.*, Page 201.

By examining the data mentioned in this table, we can come to the following conclusions:

(a) The overall ratio of Saudi teachers to the total number of teachers in the intermediate state was 36% in the year 1394/95 A.H. This percentage came down to 9·6% in the following year. The ratio of Saudi teachers to the total number of teachers of religion, Arabic, Arabic and religion, maths, science, physical education and art education has decreased in varying degrees fluctuating between 1·7 and 37·4 (as is evident from the table).

(b) The relatively small increase in the percentage of Saudi teachers of English, social sciences and maths does not meet the ever-growing need for enough Saudis to teach these subjects. Furthermore, the ratio of Saudi teachers to the total number of teachers of English and maths is basically very small. In English it did not reach more than 5% in 1394/95 A.H. whereas in maths it never exceeded 10·7% in the same year.

(c) It is worth mentioning here that despite the fact that Saudi teachers in intermediate schools totalled 1768 in 1394/95 A.H. 1055 of these teachers do not have any educational diploma. In other words, 59% of the total number of Saudi teachers at the intermediate stage are not educationally qualified to take up the teaching profession.[3] In addition to what has been mentioned above, Saudi teachers of physical education and art are not, in most cases, university graduates.[4]

(2) *In the Secondary Stage*

As far as secondary school education is concerned, the ratio of Saudi teachers to the total number of secondary school teachers is indeed much worse than that at the intermediate stage. The following table is a clear proof of this phenomenon.

Table 2

Distribution of teachers in secondary schools and the percentage of the Saudis in accordance with school subjects:

Subject	Total Number	Number of Saudis	% of Saudis to Total Number	Total Number	Number of Saudis	% of Saudis to Total Number	% of Rise or Fall
Religion	134	84	63	156	83	53·2	9·8−
Arabic Language	265	50	19	331	45	13·6	5·4−
Arabic & Religion	10	1	10	16	1	6·3	3·7−
English	241	5	2·1	277	10	3·6	1·5+
Social Sciences	179	60	33·5	184	58	31·5	2 −
Maths	189	14	7·4	216	17	7·9	·5+
Physical Sciences	246	14	5·7	338	14	4·1	1·6−
Sciences & Maths	19	1	5·3	6	—	nil	5·3
Physical Education	50	10	20	60	5	8·3	11·7−
Art Education	24	1	4	. . .	. . .		
Behavioural Subjects	1	—	nil	. . .	. . .	. . .	
	1358	240	17·7	1584	233	14·7	3−

. . . = unavailable data
The data mentioned in this table are quoted from the two previous references.

After a thorough examination of the data mentioned in this table, the following facts are easily detected:

(a) Obviously the overall ratio of Saudi teachers to the total number of secondary school teachers is certainly very low. It was 17·7% in 1394/95 A.H.; then came down to 14·7% in 1395/96 A.H.

(b) The percentage of Saudi teachers of English, maths, and science and maths is extremely low.

(c) It is quite noticeable that although the ratio of Saudi teachers to the total number of teachers was low; to begin with it was reduced in one year in varying degrees fluctuating between 11·7% and 1·6%. The only increase was in the teachers of English and maths., an increase which reached 1·5% and ·5% respectively. Yet such an increase is insufficient particularly if we realize that it did not exceed 3·6% in 1395/96 A.H.

Moreover, out of the total number of Saudi teachers, which was 240 in 1394/95 A.H., 119 teachers do not have any educational qualification. In other words 49·6% of the total number of Saudi teachers at the secondary stage are not educationally qualified to practise the teaching profession.

(3) *Secondary Teacher-Training Institutes*

The situation of Saudi teachers in teacher-training institutes is not any better than that of secondary school teachers, as is evident from the statistical data in the table on page 182.

The statistical data mentioned in Table 3 indicate the following facts:

(a) Generally, the percentage of Saudi teachers in relation to the total number of teachers working in teacher-training institutes is very low for it did not rise above 17·6% in 1394/95 A.H. Very small though this percentage is, it came down to 15·5% in the following year.

(b) Not a single Saudi teacher in teacher-training institutes teaches English, mathematics or vocational subjects, and the percentage of Saudis teaching other subjects is very low indeed.

(c) Out of the total number of Saudi teachers, which was 139 in 1394/95 A.H., 44 teachers are not educationally qualified to practise teaching. In other words 31·7% of the total numbers of Saudi teachers in teacher-training institutes do not have any educational qualification.

Table 3

Distribution of teachers in Teacher-Training Institutes and percentage of Saudi teachers in accordance with the subjects taught.

Subject	1394/95 A.H.			1395/96 A.H.			% of Rise or Fall
	Total Number	Number of Saudis	% of Saudis to Total Number	Total Number	Number of Saudis	% of Saudis to Total Number	
Religion	90	33	36·7	95	33	34·7	2 —
Arabic Language	111	4	3·6	117	3	2·6	1 —
Arabic & Religion	6	—	—	4	—	—	. . .
English	35	—	—	47	—	—	. . .
Social Sciences	108	17	15·7	107	22	20·6	4·9+
Maths	70	1	1·4	82	—	—	. . .
Physical Sciences	89	5	5·6	110	4	3·6	2 —
Maths & Sciences	3	—	—	2	—	—	. . .
Physical Education	48	2	4·2	61	4	6·6	24 +
Vocational Subjects	18	5	27·8	10	—	—	. . .
Behavioural Subjects	130	71	54·6	127	61	48	6·6—
Total	791	139	17·6	837	130	15·5	2·1—

· · · = unavoidable data.
The data mentioned in this table are quoted from the two previous references.

    The above-mentioned data and remarks illustrate the present situation of Saudi teachers at the intermediate, secondary and teacher-training stages of education. Such a deplorable situation does not, in any possible way, further the aims and objectives of the Kingdom in preparing young people to teach in various educational institutions and in giving them the hope that the day will come when full or relatively full self-sufficiency in all fields and areas of specialization will be achieved. It is worth mentioning in this respect that the Kingdom's need for more and more teachers at all stages of education will be more urgent in the forthcoming years. The second development plan, now being carried out in the Kingdom, has emphasized the urgency and necessity of having more teachers. This is evident from the following table:

Table 4

Expected rise in the number of teachers in intermediate, secondary and teacher-training institutes within the years 1394/95–1400 A.H.

Stage of Education	Number of Teachers in 1394/95 A.H.	Number of Teachers in 1399/1400 A.H.	Percentage Increase
Intermediate	4953	10112	104%
Secondary	1353	2879	113%
Teacher-training	698	968	39%
Total	7004	13959	99%

Second Development Plan

It is worth noting in this respect that some Saudi teachers have abandoned teaching and preferred other activities and professions. The educational centre established at the university of Riyadh has been engaged in drawing up a plan to look into this dangerous phenomenon, discover its original causes and prescribe suitable remedies to overcome the obstacles in the way of self-sufficiency. Strenuous efforts in this field are still being made.

The Role of Faculties of Education In Teacher-Training

In our belief, faculties of education in Saudi Arabia must have a serious and specific role to play in order to overcome the shortage of Saudi teachers. They should produce sufficient and efficient teachers who are competent enough to bear the responsibilities of teaching.

It is worth mentioning that senior authorities in government have doubled the number of faculties of education throughout the Kingdom. Yet enrolments in faculties of education have clearly dwindled in the last few years. This sad fact is reflected in the number of junior freshmen in the faculty of education, Riyadh University, which totalled 405 in 1394/95 A.H. In 1395/96 A.H. the number came down to 222 and in 1396/97 A.H. was reduced to 187 students in the first semester.

In order to tackle the present situation we must investigate the role of the faculties of education in training intermediate and secondary school teachers, besides those who graduate from teacher-training institutes.

In our enquiry we should briefly refer to the basic components which make up an efficient teacher. In the light of innumerable investigations into the measurement of the teacher's effectiveness the total personality of the teacher and its constituent aspects should be closely considered.[5]

(1) *The Physical Aspect*

The teacher's physical constitution must be healthy and free from any physical disability or deformity which might hinder him from performing his job in the best possible manner. He must be able to put up with the hardships and inconveniences of the teaching profession. Therefore, a medical examination is indispensable before any student is admitted into faculties of education. And even after being admitted students of these faculties should receive proper medical care until they graduate. Student medical care should be the main responsibility of all deans of students' affairs.

(2) *The Social and Psychological Aspect*

Studies in this field indicate that the efficient teacher is characteristically one who has certain social and psychological features. He must above all be emotionally stable, affectionate to his pupils, committed to the morals of his profession, dignified and unashamed of being a teacher, able to lead and guide his pupils, and inwardly motivated to perform his duties. In his behaviour and moral principles the efficient teacher must set the best example to his pupils.

184

(3) *The Mental and Cognitive Aspect*

Since the promotion of the mental effectiveness of pupils and raising the standard of their social adaptability are the ultimate objectives of education, the teacher must be highly qualified to help his pupils grow mentally; consequently he must fully assimilate the teaching material, have a good, strong grasp of his national culture, and be closely familiar with contemporary achievements in almost all fields. He must be able to activate the mental abilities of his pupils, enrich their imaginative powers and widen the scope of their interests.

(4) *The Vocational Aspect*

Education is truly an applied science. Hence it is a science of performance. Performance subjects usually involve the search for better ways and means of securing a higher performance in practical situations. Therefore, an efficient teacher must be acquainted with various branches of knowledge. He must acquire and develop several skills which might help him undertake the heavy responsibilities of teaching. Not irrelevant to the teacher's individual potentialities, skills and endowments is his knowledge of the importance of education in social development, and the distinctive psychological features of learners at different stages of education. Moreover, he must acquire skills which have proved indispensable for the success of the teaching process. He must be skilful in evaluating the progress of his pupils and remedying their weaknesses which often affect their school achievement.

Having briefly reviewed the distinctive characteristics of the efficient teacher let us discuss the role of faculties of education in training Saudi teachers. In our belief, faculties of education should undertake the following responsibilities:

(1) *The Selection of Students*

Only secondary school graduates and some graduates of the secondary teacher-training institutes find their way into faculties of education. The first group, though relatively small in number, can avail them-

185

selves of many opportunities to pursue university education in faculties other than those of education. They can, upon immediate graduation from secondary schools, work in various government departments or engage in free commercial enterprises. This means that there is no balance between supply and demand, for in this particular situation the demand is much greater than the supply. In training prospective teachers, faculties of education should bear this fact in mind and work out their programmes accordingly. They should, in collaboration with secondary schools, launch an immediate campaign to tempt secondary school students and make them less reluctant, to join faculties of education. Every means of communication should be shrewdly and effectively employed in this campaign, the ultimate aim being the students' consciousness of the ever-growing importance of education in bringing about social refinement, progress and self-realization for both teachers and students. The campaign should also aim at acquainting students with the various scientifc and social activities on which teacher-training programmes are based, as well as with the material and social gains with which teachers are rewarded. In this campaign no effort should be spared to make students fully aware of the role of education in bringing about social progress and refinement. Rhetoric, lecturing or one-way communication should be abandoned in planning this campaign. The whole plan should basically depend on discussion and dialogue; it should endeavour to change the negative attitudes some students may have towards the teaching profession.

(2) *The Programmes of Faculties of Education*

Students of faculties of education are overloaded with programmes and courses because of the strong competition between teachers of specialized courses and those responsible for teaching practice and methodology. Students are torn between the two sides and do not know where they stand. They are at a loss, particularly when each side thinks that its work is inspired by the ultimate objective of the teacher-training plan. It is high time that the three pivotal approaches to teacher-training should be reconciled. In other words, students should be widely cultured, professionally efficient and sufficiently trained in the field of specialization.

Those who plan and conduct all aspects of teacher-training should pay greater attention to the following considerations:

186

(a) Specialized human knowledge is increasing year after year both quantitively and qualitatively. This ever-increasing wealth of human knowledge calls for teacher training programmes which are mainly concerned with the fundamentals of specialized subjects.

(b) Vocational and educational training has become an indispensable factor in the teaching process at all levels of education and even at the university. Both Cairo and Ain Shams universities in the Arab Republic of Egypt have deemed it necessary for every teacher to attend and pass a teacher-training course before becoming a staff-member in any department or faculty. These teacher-training courses are prescribed for demonstrators and assistant teachers in every area of specialization before they are accepted as university staff-members.

(c) Intermediate and secondary school teachers should be well acquainted with their national culture and at the same time with contemporary culture.

In the light of the above-mentioned considerations and in view of the limited four-year period which students spend at faculties of education, teacher-training programmes should be periodically revised and reconsidered. Revision and reconsideration should, in the first place, aim at eliminating all irrelevant material, over-lapping and outdated subject-matter. Teacher-training courses must be regarded as the starting-point in the preparation of students for the teaching profession. 'Continuous education', which we shall deal with later in this study, should be applied in faculties of education.

If teachers are called upon to expand the mental potentialities of the learners, faculties of education should, through well planned and up-to-date programmes, increase the mental effectiveness of prospective teachers. To achieve this end, teacher-training courses should not be conducted through the old, traditional lecturing and dictating methods. Teaching staffs in faculties of education should rely on discussion and argument; they should train students in research and assess them in the light of the individual studies that the students have themselves made.

In teacher-training programmes faculties of education should attach greater importance to teaching-practice. Methods and patterns of teaching practice should be diversified; they should not be restricted to the old traditional pattern in which the student, having given a certain lesson, meets with his colleagues and supervisor for criticism, guidance and evolution. In order to improve methods and patterns of teaching practice the following suggestions are offered:

(a) Micro-teaching methods should be adopted.
(b) Teachers supervising practical training should, now and then, conduct model lessons, from observing which, students can improve their own teaching performance.
(c) Students should be drilled in setting objective tests in the subjects they are teaching.
(d) In the course of practical training students should participate in school cultural, scientific and sports activities.
(e) Educational films should be shown so that students may have the chance to imitate models of good teaching performance.

In order to make Saudi youth more desirous of entering the teaching profession and to encourage them to prefer it to any other profession, medical, social and financial facilities should be provided to students of faculties of education throughout their years of study. These facilities should be extended to the teachers as well. To achieve this, faculties of education should:

(i) Give substantial financial rewards to students of faculties of education far exceeding those granted to students in other faculties.
(ii) Provide unpaid accommodation and living facilities to students.
(iii) Organize educational excursions for students inside and outside the Kingdom, the aim of which would be to widen the scope of the students, culture and link it with contemporary cultural achievements. These excursions could be organized in summer vacations or inter-semester holidays.
(iv) Allow students free access to reference works and textbooks.
(v) Grant brilliant and distinguished students monetary rewards.
(vi) Extend to students preventative and medical care and provide them with leisure facilities.

(3) The Follow-up of New Teachers

Faculties of education will have made a serious mistake if they think their role in training prospective teachers should be halted immediately upon the graduation of students. Carefully planned objective studies have proved that the first years of teaching are the most critical, for during these years young teachers recognize their true role and acquire the basic principles of the teaching profession. They will have adopted methods and criteria which will influence and mould their behaviour for many years to come.[5]

In fact the young teacher, while practising in schools, is confronted with an atmosphere completely dissimilar to that in which he was trained to be a teacher. He has to work with older and long-experienced teachers who may have a completely different attitude from his: to students, methods of teaching and evaluation, and to the teaching profession in general. The imminent danger in this case lies in that the new teacher may find himself a stranger in the school environment, unable to adapt to school life. Very often this adaptability will be at the expense of knowledge and skills, values and methodologies that the faculties of education have striven to inculcate in the minds of their graduates.

Hence it has been thought necessary for faculties of education throughout the Kingdom, in collaboration with the Ministry of Education, to follow up all newly graduated teachers. This follow-up can be done in many ways, such as:

(a) A special unit can be established in every faculty of education to follow up graduates and provide them with journals, periodicals, book-reviews and research findings and any other material that will help consolitdate their professional experience. This follow-up unit will help sustain the students' commitment to the values and attitudes which faculties of education have painstakingly engraved on their minds. It will also welcome their views, help them better to visualize the problems and difficulties with which they are confronted and to suggest solutions to them.

(b) Each faculty of education can organize an annual symposium for its graduates who should themselves suggest topics for discussion.

(c) Faculties of education can ensure that their graduates partici-

pate in research (particularly field research) devised and
conducted by educational research centres.

(4) *Improving Teachers' Working Conditions*

We have previously referred to the profound significance of education
as a motive force in enabling society to achieve its ultimate goals. We
have also emphasized the teacher's role as the decisive factor in the
success and effectiveness of the learning process. In view of this we
can safely say that to give adequate support to teachers in their
important task the state should make them feel economically, socially
and psychologically secure. Here are some of the ways in which this
can be done:

(a) A substantial increase in salary should be given to every teacher
in appreciation of the heavy and innumerable responsibilities
of the teaching profession.

(b) The Ministry of Education should select distinguished teachers
and promote them so that they are encouraged not to give up
teaching in preference to another profession or job.

(c) The minimum period before there can be promotion to a higher
grade should be shortened.

(d) Teachers working in outlying areas should be paid a substantial
allowance in addition to their salaries.

(e) Teachers working away from home should be suitably and
decently accommodated.

(f) Distinguished teachers should be sent abroad or to other parts
of their country to carry on studies related to teaching and
teaching methods. They should be allowed easy access to
professional or specialized post-graduate studies.

(g) The mass media should inculcate positive attitudes towards
teaching among all strata of society.

(h) The Ministry of Education should call upon teachers to take an
active part in making decisions in those educational and
administrative affairs which are closely concerned with the
nature of the teaching profession.

(i) The years a teacher spends in a faculty of education should be added to those devoted to actual teaching when his retirement date is fixed.

The ideas and suggestions embodied in this study represent the views of those who prepared it, and they are put forward for further discussion, analysis and investigation. May Allah Guide us in our deliberations.

(*Translated* from Arabic by
Muhammad Abdul Majid Barghout)

NOTES

1. E. A. Robinson and I. E. Vaizy: *The Economic of Education* (London: Macmillan Co., 1969).
2. Organization for Economic and Development. *Policy Conference on Economic Growth and Investment in Education* (Washington D.C., 1961).
3. Ministry of Education: *Efficiency level of Teachers in General Education Stages and General Teacher-Training Institutes in 1394/95 A.H. (P. 14)*.
4. *Ibid.*
Statistical data quoted from the two previous references (Pages 16 & 253).
5. Robert N. Bush 'The Formative Years in the Real World of the Beginning Teacher' (Washington D.C.: N.E.A. 1965, PP. 1–14).

Chapter Six

Reconstruction of Curriculum for the Muslim Teacher

Abdul Ghafur Chaudhri
Ghulam Nabi Saqib

Professor Abdul Ghafur Chaudhri worked as a Professor of Islamic Education at the Central Training College, Lahore and then as the Principal of the Training College, Faisalabad, Pakistan. He retired as Director-General of the West Pakistan Board of School Text Books. He was also a member of the Zakir Hussain Committee for Curriculum and the member of the Executive Committee for the implementation of Islamic Culture. Publications include: *Islamic Education in the World Perspective*, Aligarh, *Some Aspects of Islamic Education*, Lahore and *Ibn Hashem, His thoughts and Methods*, Lahore.

Dr. Ghulam Nabi Saqib was born 1929, in Pakistan, Pakistani; British; Graduation and Teaching Degree from University of the Punjab, Lahore. Academic Diploma in Education; M. Phil; and Ph.D. from University of London Institute of Education. Field of specialization, comparative education with special reference to Muslim education and modernization. Previously, teacher and then Lecturer under the Inner London Education Authority between 1960–66; Taught English at King Abdulaziz Secondary School Mecca 1966–70; Assistant Professor, King Abdulaziz University, Mecca 1974 to date. Assistant Secretary of London Institute of Education; Assistant Secretary, First World Conference on Muslim Education, King Abdulaziz University, Mecca. Publications include: *Modernization of Muslim Education: A comparative Study of Egypt, Pakistan and Turkey*, London, 1977; 'The Muslim Approach to Comparative Education', *Proceedings of Workshops on Comparative Education*, Jawaharlal Nehru University, New Delhi; 'Aspects of the Organization, Finance and Administration of Teacher Education', *Fifth General Meeting of the Comparative Education Society of Europe*, Stockholm, 1971; 'Modernization of the Muslim Society and Education: Need for a practical Approach', *Education and Society*, London, 1980. Languages known: English, Arabic, Persian and Urdu.

Introduction

The teacher has been assigned a pivotal position in Muslim Society. His function is not confined merely to instructing and training Muslim youth in the prescribed subjects and skills but he has to act as a model

192

and to inculcate among his students the norms of behaviour and values prescribed in Islam. His role, therefore, transcends his social functions. He has a vital spiritual and moral involvement besides the social. His intellectual and professional attainments are essential to his task but his moral and spiritual standing and his conduct are of paramount importance for character building and the training of his pupils in Islam. It is in this context that Islam considers the teacher's role similar to that of the Prophet. Therefore, it follows that when Muslim Society suffers from a moral crisis its schools and teachers directly manifest the symptoms of its degeneration. Such exactly is the position now. The Muslim teacher has himself lost a sense of direction, so he fails to guide Muslim youth to the desired ideals.

The Problem

The basic problem of our educational system, judging from the Islamic point of view, is that it does not stand on its own ideological feet. About two centuries of alien rule in the larger part of the Muslim world have sown in the students seeds of intellectual and moral inferiority. Dogmas and values which reflect alien norms and lifestyles and often run counter to Islamic values have been implanted into our culture without regard to their over-all effect. The result is an inevitable means-ends conflict within our society, a loss of faith in our own ethical systems and the idealization of secular concepts which prove disastrous to Islamic society.

Teacher education in particular in Muslim countries suffers from this malaise. We often look to the West for guidance and inspiration in teacher education but are filled with dismay when we find that teacher education in Europe and America is not given a high priority and the teacher has a low status in the economic and social scale. To illustrate the point let us look at some views on teacher education in Western societies.

According to Robert Spillan, 'Teacher education is the form of professional training least respected by professionals and the general public. Few teachers believe that their expertise was gained in education courses. Few parents concede that the teachers have special access to an esoteric body of knowledge.' This statement is supported by a study of Schools of Education which suffer by comparison with other University Schools.

Similar views about Teacher education were expressed in the British Education Year Book 1971–1972, which maintained. 'Training colleges in the U.K. were small, closed, isolated and inward looking units. The curriculum was limited to what its students were likely to teach. The regime was illiberal, restrictive and authoritative. The course was a two-year intellectual imprisonment'.

The McNair Report of 1944 was a serious indictment of training institutions in the U.K. It condemned the 'trail of cheapness' about the college course in the training institutions.

In the U.S. the National Study Commission on Undergraduate Education and the Education of the Teachers has something disparaging to say about the quality of the candidates seeking admission to the Training Institutions i.e. persons, 'who want an extra course for credit or salary; also housewives who want to get back to work'.

These views confirm that the teaching profession has suffered both in status and standards, a deterioration which has continued unabated and without any sign of recovery. This failure has acquired more alarming dimensions in the developing countries, a category to which most of the Muslim countries belong. Here there has been an explosion in school populations and a phenomenal expansion of educational systems following the gaining of independence. This expansion broke the bounds of any organized control because the main drive was political, and not educational. The resultant shortage of teachers created a relaxation in the conditions of training. A natural outcome was a scaling down of standards in all spheres of training.

Another cause which affected the quality of prospective teachers was a change in the career expectancy of the teaching profession. Under colonial rule, the main stream of educated youth of the middle class was directed into teaching and it absorbed the majority. For the colonial power, it appeared a safe diversion for the aspirations of local youth.

But as a result of the growth and development which took place as an aftermath of Independence, teaching, hitherto the only channel for graduates, was low on the list of potential vocations. Other jobs, more challenging and socially significant entered the field in competition with teaching. They were frequently more rewarding in opportunities also. Even in developed countries like the U.S.A. according to the Lloyd Warner Status scale, neither the high school teacher nor the grade school teacher appears in the top occupational scale. In the United Kingdom according to a survey of the National Union of

Teachers, 'The picture of the teacher which emerged was in some aspects highly unflattering, being that as a group, they did not merit a higher reward than they were currently receiving.'

With the degradation of the teacher on the social scale there has been a corresponding diminution of the position, status and the quality of the training institutions. Similarly, educational research has not been able to get off the ground. During its brief history, there has been hardly any sense of achievement. Its focal point has been constantly oscillating from one position to another. There was hardly any comprehensive outlook on research and enquiry.

In the beginning the 'Master' of methodology ruled the scene. He was replaced after some time by the psychologist and the sociologist. Even the anthropologist had his heyday for some time and finally the boat stranded on the rock of curriculum construction where it has stayed ever since. There has been some attempt at research into practice teaching but it is still in a very elementary stage.

To sum up, there has been an overall decline of the teacher: his status in society, his background education and any research into improving his professional efficiency and progress. The whole question forms a part of the crisis which is symptomatic of the confusion of values at the present time. This state of affairs deeply vexes the Muslim educational reformer since his own education and cultural heritage possesses richer and nobler traditions of the teacher and his education.

The traditional Islamic system of education combined a moderate income with tremendous earnestness and professional competency. In the first place teaching was a calling for the teacher and not a professional career or business proposition. His work was abundantly rewarding for him personally and for the unsurpassed social prestige which it brought in its wake. To quote an example, in the seating order at the royal court, the teacher had precedence over all other social classes. The teachers in higher institutions attained the heights of social and moral eminence, while in the rural areas the village teacher was the leader of the village and his influence embraced all aspects of the life of the community.

He was an adviser for the village Council of Elders, the master of ceremonies for social functions like a wedding or a festival. In most cases he enjoyed a land grant which went from father to son or a stipulated share in the annual crop.

Traditions die hard even in adversity. In spite of the devastating incursion of Western influence upon Muslim societies thousands of teachers in schools of Islamic education still cherish these traditions. But can they be revived so as to produce a viable synthesis of the old and the new, the traditional and the modern norms of education?

The Quest for Model Muslim Teachers

Urgently needed for the revival of Islamic education are model Muslim teachers who, thoroughly grounded in the religion and culture of Islam, can, by conviction and practice of the Islamic way of life, set examples of Muslim character (as in the golden age of Islam) for their pupils.

It is vital that a new scheme of training be devised through which the Muslim teacher of today has primarily, intensive training in the fundamentals of Islam but also receives training in other modern branches of learning. To achieve this it is necessary to amass knowledge from the Islamic point of view and draw up a new curriculum for teachers. We have not merely to reconstruct and re-cast the curriculum but prepare the basic foundations. It is with this end in view that an attempt has been made in the following pages to introduce a model curriculum for the training of the Muslim teacher.

Normative Guidelines for Teacher Education

Muslim Education derives its norms from the Quran and the Sunnah i.e. the Life and Teachings of Prophet Muhammad (peace be upon him). Any ideal that fails to conform to these sources must be considered extraneous to Islam.

Islam is a unitarian creed par excellence. The concept of Tawhid (monotheism) or Unity or Reality permeates and governs all aspects of Muslim life and culture. Tawhid is the *elan vital* of Muslim education. So its philosophy and epistemology and its institutional framework are all regulated by this exiological concept which generates basic principles some of which are highlighted here.

The Principle of the Unity of Knowledge

Expressed in epistemological terms, Tawheed implies that there is an essential unity in all knowledge. There is no dichotomy between the religious and the secular or the intuitive and the intellectual. As the great twentieth century thinker Iqbal has pointed out, intellect and intuition are not opposed to one another: the one grasps reality piecemeal, the other grasps it in its wholeness. 'The one fixes its gaze on the eternal, the other on the temporal aspect of reality — both are needed for mutual rejuvenation. Both seek visions of the same reality which reveals itself to them in accordance with their function in life. In fact intuition, as Bergson rightly says, is only a higher kind of intellect.' That is why all means of acquiring knowledge — intellect, emotion sensation and spirit are interrelated. This interrelationship is established only when these other means accept the direction of the human spirit and do not assert their own independence. In the West man has allowed these different means complete independence. As a result, the validity of what is acquired through the intellect is not tested by the norm received by the Spirit. This spiritual norm is given to man by Allah through the revelations sent through Prophet Muhammad (peace be on him) and enshrined in the Quran; and through Allah's chosen man — the same Prophet (peace be on him) whose sayings and actions are regarded by Allah as the supreme example for man. That is why even the conclusions reached by scientists and their methodology can be considered invalid if they contradict that which has been revealed in the Quran and the Sunnah. They have not been able to collect all necessary data. Similarly literature which makes man accept and applaud the destruction of basic values, which the Quran and Sunnah assert, will also be regarded as pernicious and hence bad.

This of course does not mean that man has already acquired all knowledge. He has available the source of complete spiritual knowledge in the Quran and the Sunnah. There cannot be any change in them because man's spirit is eternally and universally the same. Allah has Himself said, 'Today I have perfected the religion for you and completed my favour upon you and have chosen Islam as your religion.' As this Islam is an all-comprehensive code of life, as the basic nature of man and the means of achieving the highest destiny — Khalifatullah (vicegerent of God) — has also been shown to human beings, man's intellect, feelings and sense — perceptions need proper discipline in order not to deviate from the path of 'purity'. It is only when intellect, emotive realization and sensations are disciplined through willing acceptance of the dominace of spirit — and this happens when a man has Faith — then, and then only, there is harmony in man. Otherwise the malaise of Western civilization — imbalance, sexual perversity, permissiveness, dry-as-dust intellectualism at the cost of emotions and feelings, or sentimentalism — would be courted by a modern Muslim.

The dominance of spirit does not prevent man from responding adequately to change in circumstances. It helps him. Man's spirit and the basic values of man do not change but circumstances do because man goes on piling knowledge on knowledge and also applying such knowledge to modify or change life. Hence there is diversification of knowledge. This diversification and accumulation of knowledge do not change man's personality or change values because his basic nature does not change. Because of changed or different circumstances, emphasis on certain aspects of human personality in one period or place may differ. But the personality, and hence the goal remains the same. The highest ideal is also the same because it is a reflection of the personality of the Prophet Muhammad (peace be on him). It is *this common ideal* for mankind that should be cultivated through teacher-training programmes.

Here is an outline of a model curriculum based on these principles.

The scheme is based on the classical division of Muslim sciences i.e. the *Fardh Ain* (essential subjects) and *Fardh Kifiya* (the optionals); the former include the Fundamentals of Islam obtaining in the Quran and Sunnah and vouchsafed in the Shariah, while the latter embrace those branches of knowledge which have been acquired by man through his intellect.

The introduction of the subjects included under Fundamentals of Islam and their teaching, demands research of a fairly intensive nature. In fact, it is mainly this aspect of the curriculum of teacher education that demands constant vigilance on the part of those responsible for its implementation.

Proposed Curriculum for
Muslim Teachers

I Essential Subjects (Revealed Knowledge)

The Teaching of Religion and
Islamic Culture

1. *Beliefs*

- (a) Tawheed
- (b) Prophethood
- (c) Al-Quran (Tajweed Tahfiz)
- (d) Morality
- (e) Metaphysics

2. *Practices*

- (a) Salat (Prayer)
- (b) Ramadhan (Fasting)
- (c) Zakat (Islamic Taxation)
- (d) Hajj (Pilgrimage)
- (e) Jihad (Crusade)

3. *Islamic Culture*

- (a) Islamic Culture and its History
- (b) Islamic Education and its History
- (c) Muslim Institutions and their Functions

(d) Modern Challenges and Muslim Movements
(e) Arabic

II Optional Subjects (Acquired Knowledge)

(a) The Teaching of Physical Sciences
(b) The Teaching of Social Sciences
(c) The Teaching of Arts and Crafts
(d) The Teaching of Languages
(e) Teaching Methods and Instructional Technology

III The Education of Women Teachers

Conclusions

I Essential Subjects

(a) General: The Teaching of Religion and Moral and Spiritual Training

The success of the entire curriculum, nay the entire plan of Education, will depend on the teaching of religion as it constitutes the very foundation of Islamic Education. The most careful attention should be paid to the teaching of this subject because it is not an exercise in memorization or learning of a language or formulas; here the pupil should imbibe the spirit of the fundamentals and acquire their emotional and spiritual essence. At present, the language and style in which religious subjects are presented are extremely formal and prosaic. But this should not be so. Teachers of religion should strive to appeal to the sensitivity with which young minds regard religious matters. The wealth of the child's emotional life and his spiritual sincerity can be a great source of strength in the case of a teacher who knows how to handle his subject psychologically and whose delivery is inspiring.

For this, the Teacher should have some insight into the richness of religious experience in people and some knowledge of the psychology of religious experience. Unless the teacher is religious himself, he cannot understand this experience.

(b) The Teaching of Beliefs and Practices

The teaching of subjects categorized under these headings is a delicate task. Basically it aims at initiation of the young into the Islamic way of life. Great skill, sincerity and dedication therefore are required of the teacher to inspire the minds and souls of children to a correct approach to religious knowledge and experience.

Some aspects of belief can be taught formally, but others need participation and practice. The entire school system and its activities have to be so organized as to promote an Islamic atmosphere in which all can participate.

The Quran

It is the sacred duty of every Muslim family to see that their children are taught the Holy Quran. This teaching task was, and is still being performed by the mosque teacher throughout the Islamic world. But secular schools in Muslim countries pay little attention to teaching the Holy Quran mostly because of the orientation of schooling developed during foreign rule. All training institutions in the Islamic world must train teachers in the correct recitation (Tajweed) of the Quran and with the same sincerity of the mosque teacher.

Preservation of the Quranic text in its perfect form has always been considered the collective duty of the Muslim Community and generation after generation of Muslims have memorized and transmitted the Holy Book to their progeny. So the memorization of the Quran (*Tahfizul* Quran) has been a fundamental subject of Muslim education.

Recently, the movement of *Tahfizul* Quran has grown in popularity and has extended its sphere of activity in all stages of the educational system. But as yet no scientific study has been made of the effect of memorizing the Quran on the general attitude, moral and intellectual, of pupils. A close survey would certainly reveal advantages which could have a profound influence in the development of both the personality of the pupil and his learning.

There is an urgent need to conduct a research project on studying those factors which help in learning the Quran and those that militate against it. Books on education give instructions in *Tahfiz* but there is also a need for discovering these factors on a scientific basis through survey and experimental work. The findings should have a place in the Teacher's Guide to teaching the Holy Quran.

(c) Islamic Culture

Before he is accepted into the teaching profession, a candidate is expected to have thoroughly studied in depth Islamic Culture: its functional and institutional aspects; its history and development down the centuries; its present-day ramifications as well as challenges. His training course should then be geared towards making him competent to teach this complex subject in such a manner that young Muslim children are well versed in their Islamic Cultural heritage and grow up to: appreciate and defend it; to promote and perpetuate it; to uphold and convey it to the next generation. The first and foremost duty of every school system is always to instil, among its young, love of its cultural heritage.

Considerable harm has already been done to the teaching of this subject in various Muslim countries and with disastrous effects. Muslim youth seem to have little knowledge of their own Culture and hence become easily vulnerable to the onslaught of alien cultural influences.

(d) Arabic

As the language of the Quran, Arabic has been the most potent vehicle of Islamic culture and a source of Islamic unity. Before the Islamic world was submerged under colonial rule and splintered into nation states where national languages gained priority in educational and cultural programmes, Arabic occupied the position of a supra-national language which bound all Muslim peoples together. One could not become an educated Muslim without having mastery of Arabic. The importance of Arabic has to be restored in the Muslim world and be given top priority in all plans of Muslim educational reform, both at national and at international levels.

In the case of Muslim countries with a non-Arabic population mother tongues such as Urdu, Persian, Turkish, Swahili, Malay, Indonesian and others, abound in words directly taken from the Quran or derivations from the Quranic vocabulary. A study of the derivatives provides enough knowledge of the grammatical structures to supply a pupil with a modicum of knowledge of the elements of Quranic grammar. Nearly all the words used in common Muslim prayers are current in the mother tongues of Muslim countries. A central institution such as the world Islamic Education Centre might organize a pilot research project for learning Arabic. The Centre could prepare a basic Arabic vocabulary. The next step would be the correlation of vocabulary and grammar structures of Arabic with mother tongues. National efforts in this direction should be coordinated and guided by the World Centre at Mecca.

II Optional Subjects

(a) Physical Sciences

The Quran constantly exhorts Muslims to study and observe the workmanship of God. The teaching of science subjects in Islam has, therefore, been given the status of *Fardh Kifaya* (a collective duty) i.e. their study is compulsory for Muslim Society as a whole and for selected members of that society, but not for every individual. According to Al-Ghazali, their importance transcends their optional status. The study of sciences was considered by Muslims to be so significant that Islam can rightly claim to have gained excellence in scientific learning and technology before the rise of Western countries. Great Muslim scientists excelled in scholarship and produced illustrious treatises on sciences which for a long time remained the only sources of scientific learning in the world. Science subjects have, therefore, great importance in the curriculum for the Muslim teacher.

The approach to the study of science subjects in a Muslim society must be based on the norms of unity of knowledge and reality. There is no dichotomy between secular and religious knowledge. Islam considers scientific knowledge as important as religion and Muslim scientists of old were the most glorious products of this unified Islamic system of learning. The life and training of Muslim scientists mirrored faithfully the Islamic outlook on science. For them, even in essentially mathematical and scientific enquiry, the Divine Will and Authority was supreme and it guided and enlightened the path towards further discoveries. They held that scientific method provided at best a knowledge of partial reality and the knowledge of the ultimate belonged only to Allah Whose Will was all-pervasive. They were men of very high intellectual calibre, professing the authority of intellect and scientific investigation; and along with academic integrity they were men of religion who expressed their deep convictions and spiritual outlook in their daily life. Their great ideals found cogent expression in their dying moments and their final testaments reveal their great faith in the Divine in furthering their intellectual interests. Umar Khayyam, for example, died during a prostration while he was performing his night prayers with these words:

'My Lord: I could not do full justice to my great obligation of knowing Thee'

Similarly, when Ibn Sina was involved in working out the solution of an abstruse problem or the details of an advanced theory, he would resort to prayers and alms-giving to the poor. So, knowledge was revealed to them by Divine guidance and through spiritual awareness. This synthesis of the spiritual and the worldly spheres of knowledge must remain the essential feature of scientific study and teaching for the Muslim teacher.

Another challenging task for the Muslim teacher and scientist is to question the hypotheses and generalizations advanced by Western scientists on the basis of their partial empirical observations in which they dissociate Divine influence from reality.

204

(b) Social Science Subjects

The same norms of unity that govern a Muslim's approach to sciences must guide his judgement when studying social sciences. The moral core of all human knowledge and particularly that dealing with social phenomena must never be lost sight of. Of special importance are subjects like history and psychology that define and explain individual and social behaviour.

The Quran has a well-defined philosophy of history which has been explained by Iqbal. 'It is one of the most essential teachings of the Quran that nations are collectively judged and suffer for their misdeeds, here and now.' The Quran repeatedly cites historical instances and urges the reader to reflect on man's past and present experience.

In the same way, the various schools of psychology that have developed in the West and whose theories mostly form the curriculum of the Muslim teacher, ought not to be accepted uncritically as they are misleading. Islam has defined man and his nature in a manner that does not find full expression in Western concepts of psychology. Muslim scholars have to interpret the concept of man and his behaviour as enshrined in the Quran.

The biography of the Prophet and those of his companions along with the lives of great mystics, provide a simple and practical knowledge of the psychology of religious experience, a branch of psychology which has special import for the curriculum of teacher education. Basing our work on the Islamic view of psychology, philosophers and educational thinkers have contributed chapters and sometimes entire volumes on *Ilm-al-Nafs* (the science of mind). Discussed in these writings are also the types of diseases of the mind, and their cures, as derived from the Quran, and the Traditions of the Prophet and the experiences of great teachers. These are simple and very practical guidelines and the Muslim teacher of today should know them before he learns about Western concepts of psychology.

(c) The Teaching of Languages

Islam is a religion with a world message and the amazing speed with which it extended its sphere of spiritual, cultural and political influence made the learning of the languages of the new converts imperative. A quickened interest in the arts and sciences of conquered peoples also produced a pressing demand to learn new languages. By the time Bait-al-Hikma was established during the early Abbasid period, the spectrum of linguistic interest extended from Chinese to Sanskrit in the East, to Greek and Latin in the West. The science of language was not neglected either and Ibn Sina was the first researcher to compose a brochure on the languages of central Asia. All these glorious traditions in language — learning should have precedence in the education of Muslim teachers in present times.

(d) Teaching Methodology and Instructional Technology

The post-war period has witnessed an explosion of modern communication media. Much has been achieved but the future holds in store tremendous possibilities of growth in depth and extension. Advanced technological devices and materials are being employed increasingly in the teaching process in advanced countries and these have made teaching more effective and interesting. The American Report on Instructional Technology envisages that in future the satellites will be the nodal points which will enable the consciousness of our grand-children to flicker like lightning back and forth across the face of this planet. They will be able to go anywhere and meet any one at any time without stirring from their homes. All knowledge will be open to them, all museums and libraries of the world will be extensions of their living rooms. Marvellous machines with unlimited information-handling capacity will be able to speak directly into their ears.

The history of Islamic education provides ample evidence of the wonderful resourcefulness and ingenuity with which the teacher formerly exploited the scanty material at his disposal. His main inspiration came most probably from the Traditions of the Holy Prophet who would often use the simplest and the commonest object for illustration.

The Muslim teacher should have no reservation in utilizing modern techniques and methods in his work. What he should have to learn is how to adopt the material to his own purposes as the inspiration is not

206

in the machine but in the man behind the machine. Whereas the Muslim teacher of the past was responsible for giving modern educationists certain educational methods and systems such as the monitorial system, the present-day Muslim teacher has become a slave to the lecture and the textbook without showing originality or enterprise. The audio-visual aids are either imported from abroad and shown in class without much correlation, or with superficial correlation, if produced locally. There is an urgent need for a co-ordination of effort in this direction at the international level. The World Centre for Islamic Education might set up a Central laboratory for the communication media, inspired by creative leadership, alive to the needs of the child mind and with an insight into the cultural resources of the local environment. National organizations could be provided with expert advice and technical assistance to produce radio, television and film programmes. Training courses, seminars and workshops could be organized from time to time to provide technologists with training in the effective use of material.

III The Education of Women Teachers

Muslims have always believed that the education of a man means the education of an individual while the education and training of a girl implies the bringing up of a whole family. Moreover, the cultural mores of a society are transmitted more effectively through its womanhood than its men. Hence the Traditions of the Prophet lay special emphasis on the education of girls and the reward for a person who brings up a girl is more abundant than in the case of a boy. Hence the most devoted attention has been paid in Muslim society to the education of girls. The result has been that the cultural and social perspective of Islam is enhanced by its glorious womanhood which has left a lasting impression on almost all sectors of the life of the community.

But this area of Islamic education appears to be under acute pressure as a result of rapid changes in the role of women that are appearing in the advanced countries of the world. Ideas of liberation and emancipation and the manner in which they manifest themselves in these countries are adversely affecting the coherence of Muslim society. It is imperative that the education of the Muslim women and the woman teacher should be so designed that all its inspiration should come from the Islamic Tradition. The hope for the preservation of the Islamic way of life and its regeneration lies in the proper Islamic education of the Muslim woman.

Conclusions

In order to Islamize the prevailing system of education in the Muslim world and to repair the damage done to Islamic culture during alien rule, the need for preparing and training the right type of Muslim teacher whose commitment to Islam, its ideology and values is paramount, cannot be over-emphasized. In the present period of crisis and transition the position of the Muslim teacher is more significant than at any other time. Today, the Muslim teacher represents the hope of Muslim society. Teaching is one of the most creative professions of mankind. The modern Muslim teacher should take up the responsibility of fostering growth and creativity through the creation of truly Islamic minds and characters. This newly-sought-after model of the Muslim teacher should be dedicated to the Islamic ideals of education and teaching. But he must at the same time be well-versed in modern systems and be able to strike a balance in favour of the primacy of Islamic norms and values. To enable him to perform that role, his own education should be based on a revised scheme of training that can be called Islamic. The current system of teacher education in Muslim countries miserably falls short of that ideal. The outline suggested above, it is hoped, may provide the basic starting point. Further research would be necessary for devising a well-considered curriculum. But that is only possible after the reclassification of knowledge and redesigning of curricula have been done and the core-curriculum defined. The curriculum for teacher education should be a part of the entire plan of reform of Islamic education.

Appendix

Recommendations of the Committee — B6 on Teacher Education

It is universally recognized that the teacher is the key person in an educational system. This applies with greater force and validity in-so-far as the Islamic system of education is concerned. The position of those who know, the righteous, is only next to that of the Prophets. Since Islamic society can be sustained and advanced only on the basis of Faith, Knowledge and Education, the role of the teacher assumes the highest importance both in the educational system and in society in general.

The teacher in Muslim society is not a mere wage-earner or a professional worker, but a committed member. His excellence does not depend only on his qualification or his knowledge; it depends upon what type of person he is in terms of his faith and belief and in terms of his conduct and character. His role transcends that of an instructor in-so-far as he becomes the mentor, teacher and guide of the younger generations.

The Committee is of the view that this key role of the teacher should guide basic policies regarding the education, recruitment and employment of teachers in Muslim countries.

There is a shortage of teachers, more so of qualified teachers, in Muslim countries. Educational development being the most crucial problem, all measures (both long-term and short-term) must be taken to make teachers available at all levels of education.

Recruitment and Selection

1. Teacher preparing institutions should deliberately extend their efforts into feeder schools to attract suitable candidates (i.e. students who may be further motivated to conceive of teaching as a profession that follows the footsteps of the Prophet).

209

2. The criteria of selection should be the candidate's commitment to Islam, intellectual-academic abilities, and physical fitness.

The Preparation of Teachers

1. A profile of a Muslim teacher should be developed through rigorous research conducted in various Muslim countries.
2. Teacher training institutes and colleges should experiment with alternative models of teacher education programmes.
3. The curriculum for teacher preparation should be based on Islamic ideology and utilize the best that the modern system of teacher education can offer within the Islamic framework.
4. The curriculum activities and relationships between different parts of the institution should be imbued with Islam.
5. The education and preparation of prospective teachers should be inspired with the ideal of community service, and teachers in-service should be given opportunities to engage themselves in voluntary community service.
6. Prospective teachers should be given the necessary knowledge, skills, and understanding to make an effective use of educational technology.

The Evaluation of Student Teachers and their Training Programmes

1. The progress of student-teachers should be continuously evaluated throughout their period of training in order that remedial measures may be provided for those who need them. Those who are unable to progress should be directed to follow other pursuits.
2. Teacher training programmes should be continuously evaluated for further improvement. Follow-up and feed-back programmes should be devised to reveal students' strengths and weaknesses and consequently to amend and improve their training.

210

In-Service Training

1. In-service training programmes should be designed to fulfil the following purposes:
   a. to enable qualified teachers to get abreast of current trends in the areas of their specialized studies, of advances in the profession, and of Islamic studies.
   b. to enable less qualified teachers to upgrade their qualifications.
2. To improve their professional competence, teachers should be given continuous opportunities to participate in seminars, training programmes, and educational conferences — local, regional and international.

Status and Recognition

1. The special role and status of teachers as mentors, leaders, and guides of the younger generations must be duly recognized. They should receive salaries, special allowances and other fringe benefits such as are commensurate with their qualifications.
2. Other incentives should be considered in order to keep teachers well satisfied, such as a suitable policy of promotion and of regular advancement.
3. The professional status of teachers should be recognized by providing them with opportunities to participate in the decision-making processes related to curriculum development and to educational administration. The social status of teachers should be enhanced by giving them certain privileges and showing them special consideration. The service conditions of teachers should be improved by providing adequate facilities for them in their educational institutions.

International Centre for Islamic Education

The Committee recommends the establishment of an International Centre for Islamic Education to perform the following important functions:
1. To train teacher-educators as leaders of educational thought and

practice in areas like public education (ta'lim aam), special education, and adult education.

2. To stimulate efforts that are being made to put educational curricula on to an Islamic basis, and encourage the production of suitable teaching materials and text-books at various educational levels.

3. To undertake research projects related to Islamic education in various Muslim countries and to circulate the results of these researches to all Muslim countries.